CCNP ONT Portable Command Guide

Scott Empson
Hans Roth

Cisco Press
800 East 96th Street
Indianapolis, IN 46240 USA

CCNP ONT Portable Command Guide

Scott Empson

Hans Roth

Published by:
Cisco Press
800 East 96th Street
Indianapolis, IN 46240 USA

Printed in the United States of America

First Printing March 2008

Library of Congress Cataloging-in-Publication Data:

Empson, Scott.
CCNP ONT portable command guide / Scott Empson, Hans Roth.
p. cm.
ISBN 978-1-58720-185-1 (pbk.)
1. Computer networks--Examinations--Study guides. 2. Internetworking (Telecommunication)--Examinations--Study guides. 3. Electronic data processing personnel--Certification. I. Roth, Hans. II. Title.
TK5105.5.E436 2008
004.6--dc22
2008005013

ISBN-13: 978-1-58720-185-1

ISBN-10: 1-58720-185-2

Warning and Disclaimer

This book is designed to provide information about the Cisco Certified Network Professional (CCNP) 642-845 Optimizing Converged Cisco Networks (ONT) exam and the commands needed at this level of network administration. Every effort has been made to make this book as complete and as accurate as possible, but no warranty or fitness is implied.

The information is provided on an "as is" basis. The authors, Cisco Press, and Cisco Systems, Inc. shall have neither liability nor responsibility to any person or entity with respect to any loss or damages arising from the information contained in this book or from the use of the discs or programs that may accompany it.

The opinions expressed in this book belong to the author and are not necessarily those of Cisco Systems, Inc.

Trademark Acknowledgments

All terms mentioned in this book that are known to be trademarks or service marks have been appropriately capitalized. Cisco Press or Cisco Systems, Inc., cannot attest to the accuracy of this information. Use of a term in this book should not be regarded as affecting the validity of any trademark or service mark.

Corporate and Government Sales

The publisher offers excellent discounts on this book when ordered in quantity for bulk purchases or special sales, which may include electronic versions and/or custom covers and content particular to your business, training goals, marketing focus, and branding interests. For more information, please contact: **U.S. Corporate and Government Sales** 1-800-382-3419 corpsales@pearsontechgroup.com

For sales outside the United States please contact: **International Sales** international@pearsoned.com

Feedback Information

At Cisco Press, our goal is to create in-depth technical books of the highest quality and value. Each book is crafted with care and precision, undergoing rigorous development that involves the unique expertise of members from the professional technical community.

Readers' feedback is a natural continuation of this process. If you have any comments regarding how we could improve the quality of this book, or otherwise alter it to better suit your needs, you can contact us through email at feedback@ciscopress.com. Please make sure to include the book title and ISBN in your message.

We greatly appreciate your assistance.

Publisher	Paul Boger
Associate Publisher	Dave Dusthimer
Cisco Representative	Anthony Wolfenden
Cisco Press Program Manager	Jeff Brady
Executive Editor	Mary Beth Ray
Managing Editor	Patrick Kanouse
Development Editor	Andrew Cupp
Project Editor	Mandie Frank
Copy Editor	Paula Lowell
Technical Editor(s)	Tami Day-Orsatti Mike Valentine
Editorial Assistant	Vanessa Evans
Designer	Louisa Adair
Composition	Mark Shirar
Proofreader	Kathy Ruiz

Americas Headquarters
Cisco Systems, Inc.
170 West Tasman Drive
San Jose, CA 95134-1706
USA
www.cisco.com
Tel: 408 526-4000
800 553-NETS (6387)
Fax: 408 527-0883

Asia Pacific Headquarters
Cisco Systems, Inc.
168 Robinson Road
#28-01 Capital Tower
Singapore 068912
www.cisco.com
Tel: +65 6317 7777
Fax: +65 6317 7799

Europe Headquarters
Cisco Systems International BV
Haarlerbergpark
Haarlerbergweg 13-19
1101 CH Amsterdam
The Netherlands
www-europe.cisco.com
Tel: +31 0 800 020 0791
Fax: +31 0 20 357 1100

Cisco has more than 200 offices worldwide. Addresses, phone numbers, and fax numbers are listed on the Cisco Website at **www.cisco.com/go/offices.**

About the Authors

Scott Empson is the Associate Chair of the Bachelor of Applied Information Systems Technology degree program at the Northern Alberta Institute of Technology in Edmonton, Alberta, Canada, where he teaches Cisco routing, switching, and network design courses in a variety of different programs—certificate, diploma, and applied degree—at the post-secondary level. Scott is also the Program Coordinator of the Cisco Networking Academy Program at NAIT, a Regional Academy covering Central and Northern Alberta. He has earned three undergraduate degrees: a bachelor of arts, with a major in English; a bachelor of education, again with a major in English/language arts; and a bachelor of applied information systems technology, with a major in network management. He currently holds several industry certifications, including CCNP, CCAI, and Network+. Prior to instructing at NAIT, he was a junior/senior high school English/language arts/computer science teacher at different schools throughout Northern Alberta. Scott lives in Edmonton, Alberta, with his wife, Trina, and two children, Zachariah and Shaelyn, where he enjoys reading and studying the martial art of Taekwon-Do.

Hans Roth is an instructor in the Electrical/Electronic Engineering Technology department at Red River College in Winnipeg, Canada. Hans has been with the college for 11 years and teaches in the both the Electronic Technology and IT areas. He has been with the Cisco Academy Program since 2000 teaching CCNP curricula. Previous to teaching, Hans spent 15 years in R&D/product development designing microcontroller-based control systems for consumer products as well as for the automotive and agricultural industries.

About the Technical Reviewers

Tami Day-Orsatti, CCSI, CCDP, CCNP, CCSP:SNPA, CISSP, ECI, EMCPA, MCT, MCSE 2000/2003: Security, is an IT networking, security, and data storage instructor for T^2 IT Training. She is responsible for the delivery of authorized Cisco, $(ISC)^2$, EMC, and Microsoft classes. She has more than 23 years in the IT industry working with many different types of organizations (private business, city and federal government, and DoD), providing project management and senior-level network and security technical skills in the design and implementation of complex computing environments.

Mike Valentine has 13 years of experience in the IT field, specializing in network design and installation. He is currently a Cisco trainer with Skyline Advanced Technology Services and specializes in Cisco Unified Communications and CCNA and CCNP classes. His accessible, humorous, and effective teaching style has demystified Cisco for hundreds of students since he began teaching in 2002. Mike holds a bachelor of arts degree from the University of British Columbia and currently holds the MCSE:Security, CCNA, CCDA, CCNP, CCVP, IPTX, QoS, CCSI #31461, C|EH and CTP certifications, and has completed the CCIE written exam.

Mike was on the development team for the *Cisco Unified Communications Architecture and Design* official courseware and is currently developing custom Unified Communications courseware for Skyline. Mike co-authored the popular *CCNA Exam Cram (Exam 640-802)*, third edition and has served as technical editor and contributor on several Cisco Press titles.

Dedications

This book is dedicated to Trina, Zach, and Shae, without whom I couldn't have made it through those long nights of writing and editing.

This book is also dedicated to the memory of my father, Ted Empson, April 24, 1940 – December 10, 2007. Good men must die, but death cannot kill their names. J'taime Papa.

—Scott

I'd like to dedicate this book to my wife Carol and daughter Tess. I am thankful for their grace and patience with me during my many hours in the basement.

I'd also like to dedicate this book to my wife Carol. I'm hopeful two dedications are worth more than one.

—Hans

Acknowledgments

Anyone who has ever had anything to do with the publishing industry knows that it takes many, many people to create a book. Our names might be on the cover, but there is no way that we can take credit for all that occurred in order to get this book from idea to publication. Therefore, we must thank the following people:

From Scott: The team at Cisco Press —once again you amaze me with your professionalism and the ability to make me look good. Mary Beth, Chris, Patrick, Drew, Mandie, Paula, and Dayna—thank you for your continued support and belief in my little engineering journal.

To my technical reviewers, Tami Day-Orsatti and Mike Valentine, thanks for keeping me on track and making sure that what I wrote was correct and relevant.

To the staff of the Cisco office here in Edmonton, thanks for putting up with me and my continued requests to borrow equipment for development and validation of the concepts in this book.

A big thank you goes to my co-author, Hans Roth, for helping me through this with all of your technical expertise and willingness to assist in trying to make my ideas a reality.

To Hans' wife and daughter, Carol and Tess, thank you for allowing Hans to help me when I was overwhelmed with the fact that I had five books to write in just over a year's time. I cannot thank you enough for letting Hans come over and play.

From Hans: I don't exactly know how many people it takes to get a book on the shelf. The content must be written and the graphics drawn, each section verified technically, each part massaged in editing, the presentation layout manipulated and re-edited, the pre-press and post-press work completed, including the many marketing efforts, and of course, the organization and patience of the editor and editorial staff. Certainly the writing part is only one effort in a large collection of efforts.

To the Cisco Press team, thank you for your patience and guidance, especially you Mary Beth.

To the technical reviewers, Tami Day-Orsatti and Mike Valentine, thanks.

Lastly I would like to thank my colleague in education and co-writer, Scott Empson. Scott's boundless energy has helped me refocus when I needed it. His positive attitude tempered with his vast experience in education and technical areas was an excellent rudder to help me stay on course, Lastly, Scott's experience with the process of writing for Cisco Press saved me from many of the "newbie" writer foibles. Thank you, Scott, for freely sharing your experience with me.

This Book Is Safari Enabled

The Safari® Enabled icon on the cover of your favorite technology book means the book is available through Safari Bookshelf. When you buy this book, you get free access to the online edition for 45 days.

Safari Bookshelf is an electronic reference library that lets you easily search thousands of technical books, find code samples, download chapters, and access technical information whenever and wherever you need it.

To gain 45-day Safari Enabled access to this book:

- Go to http://www.informit.com/onlineedtion.
- Complete the brief registration form
- Enter the coupon code KGDN-U2NC-5ZLL-MTC8-UXYN

If you have difficulty registering on Safari Bookshelf or accessing the online edition, please e-mail customer-service@safaribooksonline.com.

Contents at a Glance

Contents

Icons Used in This Book

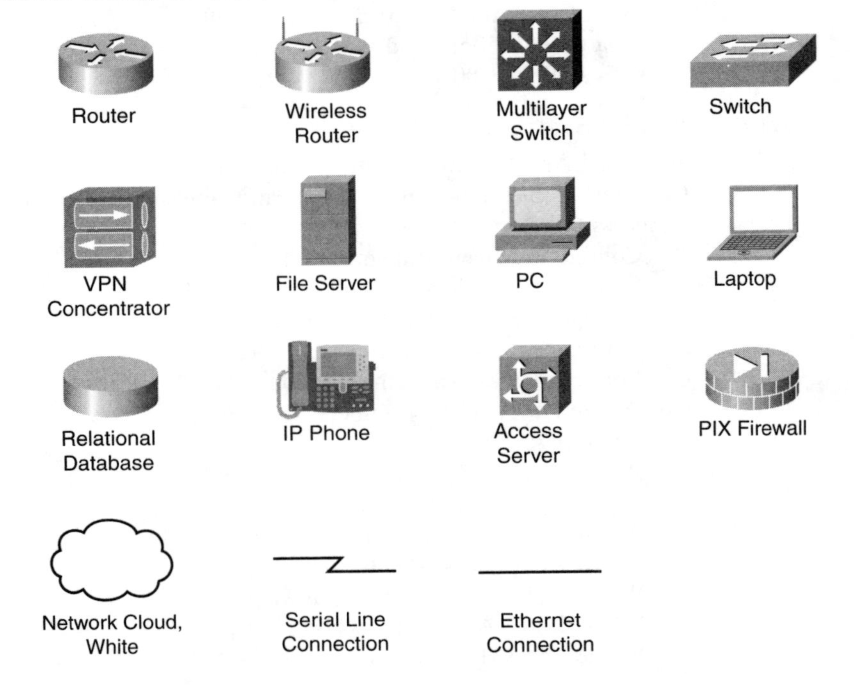

Command Syntax Conventions

The conventions used to present command syntax in this book are the same conventions used in the IOS Command Reference. The Command Reference describes these conventions as follows:

- **Boldface** indicates commands and keywords that are entered literally as shown. In actual configuration examples and output (not general command syntax), boldface indicates commands that are manually input by the user (such as a **show** command).
- *Italic* indicates arguments for which you supply actual values.
- Vertical bars (|) separate alternative, mutually exclusive elements.
- Square brackets ([ ]) indicate an optional element.
- Braces ({ }) indicate a required choice.
- Braces within brackets ([{ }]) indicate a required choice within an optional element.

Introduction

Welcome to ONT! In 2006, Cisco Press came to me and told me, albeit very quietly, that there was going to be a major revision of the CCNP certification exams. Then they asked whether I would be interested in working on a command guide in the same fashion as my previous books for Cisco Press: the Cisco Networking Academy Program *CCNA Command Quick Reference* and the *CCNA Portable Command Guide*. The original idea was to create a single-volume command summary for all four of the new CCNP exams. However, early on in my research I quickly discovered that there was far too much information in the four exams to create a single volume; that would have resulted in a book that was neither portable nor quick as a reference. So when I jokingly suggested that they let me author four books—one for each exam—who would have expected Cisco Press to agree? Well, you have to be careful for what you wish for, as Cisco Press readily agreed. Realizing that this was going to be too much for one part-time author to handle, I quickly got my colleague Hans Roth on board as a co-author.

This book is the fourth and final volume in a four-volume set that attempts to summarize the commands and concepts that you need to know in order to pass one of the CCNP certification exams—in this case, the Optimizing Converged Cisco Networks (ONT) exam. It follows the format of my previous books, which are in fact a cleaned-up version of my own personal engineering journals— a small notebook that can be carried around and that contains little nuggets of information— commands that you forget, the IP addressing scheme of some remote part of the network, and little reminders about how to do something you only have to do once or twice a year, but that is vital to the integrity and maintenance of your network.

With the creation of two brand-new CCNP exams, the amount of new information out there is growing on an almost daily basis. There is always a new white paper to read, a new Webinar to view, another slideshow from a Networkers session that was never attended. The engineering journal can be that central repository of information that won't weigh you down as you carry it from the office or cubicle to the server and infrastructure room in some branch office.

To make this guide a more realistic one for you to use, the folks at Cisco Press have decided to continue with an appendix of blank pages—pages that are for you to put your own personal touches—your own configs, commands that are not in this book but are needed in your world, and so on. That way this book will hopefully look less like the authors' journals, but more like your own.

Networking Devices Used in the Preparation of This Book

To verify the commands that are in this book, many different devices were used. The following is a list of the equipment used in the writing of this book:

- C2620 router running Cisco IOS Software Release 12.3(7)T, with a fixed Fast Ethernet interface, a WIC-2A/S serial interface card, and an NM-1E Ethernet interface
- C2811 ISR bundle with PVDM2, CMME, a WIC-2T, FXS and FXO VICs, running 12.4(3g) IOS
- C2821 ISR Bundle with HWICD 9ESW, a WIC-2A/S, running 12.4(16) Advanced Security IOS
- WS-C3560-24-EMI Catalyst switch, running 12.2(25)SE IOS
- WS-C3550-24-EMI Catalyst switch, running 12.1(9)EA1c IOS
- WS-C2960-24TT-L Catalyst switch, running 12.2(25)SE IOS
- WS-C2950-12 Catalyst switch, running version C2950-C3.0(5.3)WC(1) Enterprise Edition software
- C1760 1FE VE 4SLOT DV Mainboard Port adapter with PVDM2, CMME, WIC-2A/S, WIC-4ESW, MOD1700-VPN with 32F/128D running c1700-bk9no3r2sy7-mz.124-15.T1
- C1751 1FE VE DV Mainboard with WIC-4ESW, MOD1700-VPN with 16F/64D running c1700-advsecurityk9-mz.124-5a
- Cisco 3640 with 32F/128DRAM memory, 3 Ethernet interfaces, 2-WIC-1T running c3640-jk9o3s-mz.124-12a
- Cisco 4402 Wireless LAN Controller
- Cisco 1131 LWAP
- Cisco Wireless Control System, version 4.2.62.0 running on a Microsoft Windows Server 2003 Enterprise Edition

These devices were not running the latest and greatest versions of IOS. Some of it is quite old.

Those of you familiar with Cisco devices will recognize that a majority of these commands work across the entire range of the Cisco product line. These commands are not limited to the platforms and IOS versions listed. In fact, these devices are in most cases adequate for someone to continue their studies beyond the CCNP level as well.

Who Should Read This Book

This book is for those people preparing for the CCNP ONT exam, whether through self study, on-the-job training and practice, study within the Cisco Academy Program, or study through the use of a Cisco Training Partner. It also includes some handy hints and tips along the way to hopefully make life a bit easier for you in this endeavor. The book is small enough that you will find it easy to carry around with you. Big heavy textbooks might look impressive on your bookshelf in your office, but can you really carry them all around with you when you are working in some server room or equipment closet somewhere?

Organization of This Book

This book follows the list of objectives for the CCNP ONT exam:

- Chapter 1, "Network Design Requirements," offers an overview of the two different design models from Cisco: the Service-Oriented Network Architecture and the Enterprise Composite Network Model.
- Chapter 2, "Cisco VoIP Implementations," describes how to set up Cisco Unified Communications Manager Express (CME) using the CLI, how to use the CLI for CME auto-configuration, how to install IP Communicator, and how to change codecs using the CLI.
- Chapter 3, "Introduction to IP QoS," describes how to configure QoS through the CLI, using Modular QoS CLI (MQC) for implementing QoS, implementing QoS using AutoQoS, and implementing and monitoring QoS using Cisco Security Device Manager (SDM).
- Chapter 4, "Implementing DiffServ," describes how to use Network-Based Application Recognition (NBAR) for classification, configuring Priority Queuing (PQ), configuring Custom Queuing (CQ), configuring Weighted Fair Queuing (WQ), configuring Class-based Weighted Fair Queuing (CBWFQ), configuring Low Latency Queuing (LLQ), configuring LLQ with Class-Based Weighted Random Early Detection (CBWRED), configuring traffic policing and shaping, and implementing QoS preclassify.
- Chapter 5, "AutoQoS," includes topics such as the phases of AutoQoS, locations where AutoQoS can be implemented, router considerations and prerequisites, and deploying AutoQoS on both routers and IOS-based Catalyst switches.
- Chapter 6, "Wireless Scalability," includes topics such as configuring wireless LAN QoS using the CLI, configuring encryption and authentication on lightweight access points, and working with Cisco wireless control systems.

Did We Miss Anything?

As educators, we are always interested to hear how our students, and now readers of our books, do on both vendor exams and future studies. If you would like to contact either of us and let us know how this book helped you in your certification goals, please do so. Did we miss anything? Let us know. Contact us at ccnpguide@empson.ca.

CHAPTER 1

Network Design Requirements

This chapter provides information concerning the following topics:

- Cisco Service-Oriented Network Architecture
- Cisco Enterprise Composite Network Model

No commands are associated with this module of the CCNP ONT course objectives.

Cisco Service-Oriented Network Architecture

Figure 1-1 shows the Cisco Service-Oriented Network Architecture (SONA) framework.

Figure 1-1 Cisco SONA Framework

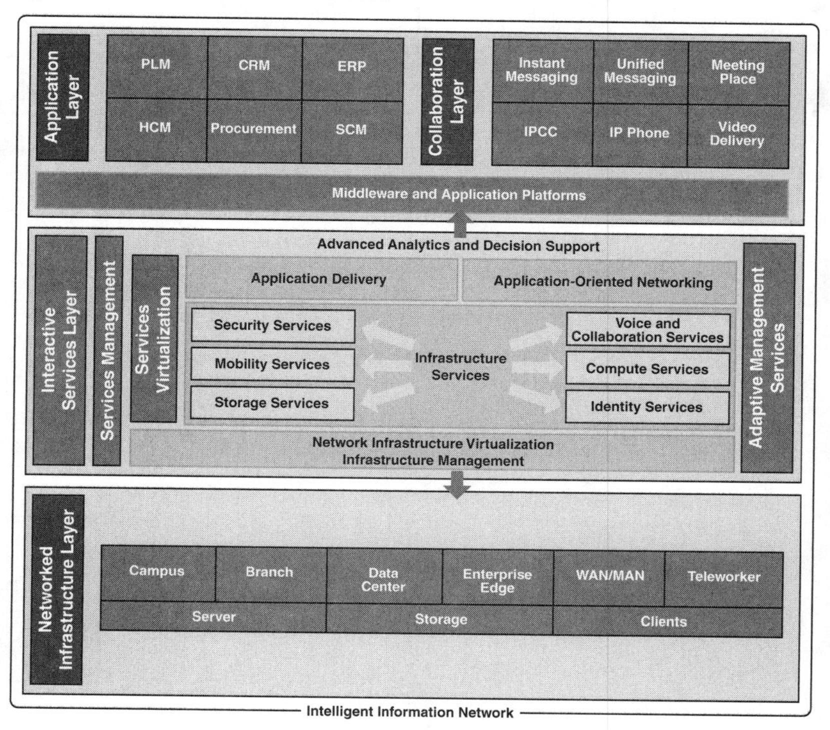

Cisco Enterprise Composite Network Model

Figure 1-2 shows the Cisco Enterprise Composite Network Model.

Figure 1-2 Cisco Enterprise Composite Network Model

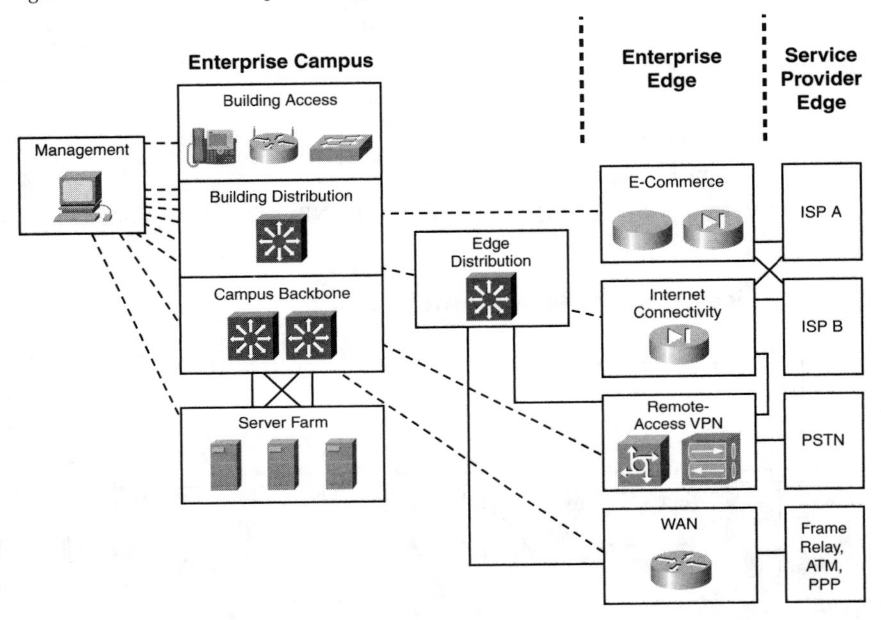

CHAPTER 2

Cisco VoIP Implementations

This chapter provides information and commands concerning the following topics:

- Cisco Unified Communications Manager Express (CME) Files
  — Moving Cisco Unified CME Files to the Router Flash
- Basic Manual CME Setup Using the CLI
  — Enabling Calls in the CME VoIP Network
  — Configuring DHCP for the VoIP Phones
  — Defining a DHCP Relay
  — Enabling Network Time Protocol
  — Creating Directory Numbers
  — Creating Phones
- CME Auto Configuration Using the CLI
- Installing IP Communicator
- Changing Codecs Using the CLI
- Router Configuration

Figure 2-1 shows the network diagram to be used as a reference for the topics covered in this chapter. The complete router configuration and the contents of the router's flash memory is given at the end of this chapter.

Figure 2-1 Cisco Unified Communications Manager Express Sample Design

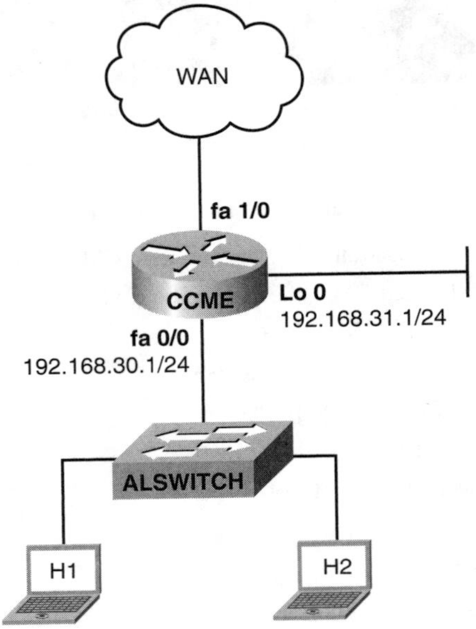

Cisco Unified Communications Manager Express (CME) Files

Cisco Unified Communications Manager Express is an IOS VoIP solution based on Cisco Integrated Services Routers. There are specific Cisco Unified CME files for each Cisco Unified CME IOS. A tar archive or zip file contains the files needed for Cisco Unified CME. Be sure to download the correct version for your hardware platform and IOS load. This tar archive or zip file typically contains the phone firmware files that you require. Check equipment and IOS compatibilities in "Cisco Unified Communication Manager Express 4.x Supported Firmware, Platforms, Memory, and Voice Products" found in the "Install and Upgrades" section of the Cisco Unified Communications Manager Express support pages at cisco.com.

The tar file does not need to be opened. The router will untar and copy the contents to the router flash maintaining the directory structure specified in the tar file.

Moving Cisco Unified CME Files to the Router Flash

`Router#` **`archive tar /xtract tftp://`** *`ip-address/tar-filename`* **`flash:`**	Uncompresses and copies each file to router flash memory.
	NOTE: Unzip the files to the TFTP server before copying to router flash.

`Router#` **`copy tftp://`***`ip-address/ filename`* **`flash:`**	Copies each file to router flash memory.
`Router(config)#` **`tftp-server flash:P0xxxxxxxxxx.bin`**	Permits TFTP access to the specified file by the IP phones.
	NOTE: Each individual Cisco CME phone firmware file requires a separate **tftp-server** command. SCCP firmware is designated by P003xxyy.bin and SIP firmware by P0S3xxyy.bin.

Basic Manual CME Setup Using the CLI

`Router(config)#` **`telephony-service`**	Enters telephony-service configuration mode.
`Router(config-telephony-service)#` **`max-ephones 24`**	Sets the maximum number of supported IP phones.
`Router(config-telephony-service)#` **`max-dn 48`**	Sets the maximum number of extensions.
	NOTE: The maximum number of phones and extensions is platform and IOS version dependent.
`Router(config-telephony-service)#` **`load 79xx P0xxxxxxxxxx`**	Identifies the Cisco IP phone firmware file to be used by specific Cisco IP phones when they register.
`Router(config-telephony-service)#` **`ip source-address 192.168.31.1`**	Identifies the IP address and port number for IP phone registration.
	NOTE: The default port is 2000.
`Router(config-telephony-service)#` **`create cnf-files`**	Builds the XML configuration files required for Cisco CME phones.
`Router(config-telephony-service)#` **`reset sequence-all`**	Resets all phones one at a time.
`Router(config-telephony-service)#` **`exit`**	Returns to global configuration mode.

Enabling Calls in the CME VoIP Network

`Router>`**`enable`**	Enables privileged EXEC mode. Enter your password if prompted.
`Router#` **`configure terminal`**	Enters global configuration mode.
`Router(config)#` **`voice service voip`**	Enters voice service configuration mode and specifies Voice over IP (VoIP) encapsulation.
`Router(config-voi-srv)#` **`allow-connections h323 to h323`**	Enables calls between specific types of endpoints in a VoIP network.
`Router(config-voi-srv)#` **`allow-connections h323 to SIP`**	Enables calls between specific types of endpoints in a VoIP network.
`Router(config-voi-srv)#` **`allow-connections SIP to SIP`**	Enables calls between specific types of endpoints in a VoIP network.
	NOTE: A separate **allow-connections** command is required for each type of endpoint to be supported.
`Router(config-voi-srv)#` **`sip`**	Enters SIP configuration mode.
	NOTE: Required if you are connecting IP phones running SIP directly in Cisco CME 3.4 and later.
`Router(config-voi-sip)#` **`registrar server expires max 600 min 60`**	Enables SIP registrar functionality in Cisco Unified CME with lowest values.
	NOTE: Cisco Unified CME does not maintain a persistent database of registration entries across CME router reloads. SIP phones will have to register again.
	NOTE: Cisco recommends setting the timers to their minimum values.

Configuring DHCP for the VoIP Phones

`Router(config)#` **`ip dhcp pool VoIP-POOL`**	Creates a name for the DHCP server address pool and enters DHCP pool configuration mode.
`Router(config-dhcp)#` **`network 192.168.30.0 255.255.255.0`**	Specifies the IP address of the DHCP address pool to be configured.

Router(config-dhcp)# **option 150 ip 192.168.31.1**	Specifies the TFTP server address from which the Cisco Unified IP phone downloads the image configuration file.
	NOTE: This is your Cisco Unified CME router's address. It is recommended to choose a loopback address.
Router(config-dhcp)# **default-router 192.168.30.1**	Specifies the gateway address for IP phone.
Router(config-dhcp)# **end**	Returns to privileged EXEC mode.
Router(config)# **ip dhcp excluded-address 192.168.30.1 192.168.30.15**	Specifies any addresses not to be dynamically allocated.

Defining a DHCP Relay

NOTE: DHCP relay is required if the Cisco Unified CME router is not the DHCP server and/or the CME router is not on a common segment with the VoIP phones.

Router(config)# **interface fastethernet 0/0**	Enters interface configuration mode for the specified interface.
Router(config-if)# **ip helper-address** *ip-address*	Specifies the IP address for any TFTP and/or DNS servers.
	NOTE: A separate **ip helper-address** command is required for each server if the servers are on different hosts. You configure multiple TFTP server targets by using the **ip helper-address** commands for multiple servers.
Router(config-if)# **end**	Returns CLI to the privileged exec prompt.

Enabling Network Time Protocol

`Router# **configure terminal**`	Enters global configuration mode.
`Router(config)# **clock timezone CST -6**`	Sets the time zone to Central Standard Time (CST), which is 6 hours behind UTC.
`Router(config)# **clock summer-time CST recurring 2 Sun Mar 2:00 1 Sun Nov 2:00**`	Optionally specifies daylight savings time.
	NOTE: If the **clock summer-time *zone* recurring** command is specified without parameters, the summer time rules default to United States rules.
`Router(config)# **ntp server** *ip-address*`	Synchronizes the software clock of the router with the specified Network Time Protocol (NTP) server.
`Router(config)# **ntp master**`	Enables the router's NTP server.
	NOTE: It is recommended to have a single authoritative timer or server that all devices and services in the network query.

Creating Directory Numbers

`Router(config)# **ephone-dn 1**`	Configures a directory number.
`Router(config-ephone-dn)# **number 1001**`	Assigns a phone number of 1001.
`Router(config-ephone-dn)# **name Bob Smith**`	Assigns a name to the directory number.

Creating Phones

`Router(config)# **ephone 1**`	Enters the ephone configuration mode.
`Router(config-ephone)# **mac-address** *HHHH.HHHH.HHHH*`	Associates the MAC address with ephone 1.
	NOTE: The address must be in the format *HHHH.HHHH.HHHH.*
`Router(config-ephone)# **type cipc**`	Configures the type of phone.

`Router(config-ephone)# button 1:1`	Assigns the first button on the phone to directory number 1.
	NOTE: The first **1** indicates the first button. The colon indicates a normal ringer. The second **1** represents directory number 1.
	NOTE: The Directory number ephone-dn 1, using phone number 1001, with the associated name "Bob Smith" is linked to ephone 1 with MAC address *HHHH.HHHH.HHHH*.

CME Auto Configuration Using the CLI

`Winnipeg(config)# telephony-service setup`	Enters CME auto-configuration mode.
Cisco IOS Telephony Services Setup:	
`Do you want to setup DHCP service for your IP Phones? [yes/no]: yes`	Enter **yes** or **no.**
Configuring DHCP Pool for Cisco IOS Telephony Services:	
`IP network for telephony-service DHCP Pool: 192.168.30.0`	Enter DHCP pool network.
`Subnet mask for DHCP network : 255.255.255.0`	Enter subnet mask.
`TFTP Server IP address (Option 150) : 192.168.31.1`	Enter TFTP server address.
`Default Router for DHCP Pool : 192.168.30.1`	Enter default router address.
`Do you want to start telephony-service setup? [yes/no]: yes`	Enter **yes** or **no.**
Configuring Cisco IOS Telephony Services:	
`Enter the IP source address for Cisco IOS Telephony Services : 192.168.31.1`	Enter source address.
`Enter the Skinny Port for Cisco IOS Telephony Services : [2000]:`	Press **Enter** for default answer of 2000.
`How many IP phones do you want to configure : [0]: 4`	Enter number of phones to configure.

`Do you want dual-line extensions assigned to phones? [yes/no]:` **`yes`**	Answer **yes** or **no.**

`What Language do you want on IP phones :`
`0 English`
`1 French`
`2 German`
`3 Russian`
`4 Spanish`
`5 Italian`
`6 Dutch`
`7 Norwegian`
`8 Portuguese`
`9 Danish`
`10 Swedish`
`11 Japanese`
`[0]:` **`0`**
	Choose the language on the phone.

`Which Call Progress tone set do you want on IP phones :`
`0 United States`
`1 France`
`2 Germany`
`3 Russia`
`4 Spain`
`5 Italy`
`6 Netherlands`
`7 Norway`
`8 Portugal`
`9 UK`
`10 Denmark`
`11 Switzerland`
`12 Sweden`
`13 Austria`
`14 Canada`
`15 Japan`
`[0]:` **`0`**
	Choose the call progress tone.

`What is the first extension number you want to configure :` **`5001`**	Enter first number.

`Do you have Direct-Inward-Dial service for all your phones? [yes/no]:` **`no`**	Answer **yes** or **no.**
`Do you want to forward calls to a voice message service? [yes/no]:` **`no`**	Answer **yes** or **no.**
`Do you wish to change any of the above information? [yes/no]:` **`no`**	Answer **yes** or **no.**
Setup completed config	

NOTE: The auto configuration does not prompt for information for individual directory numbers and phone specifics. The auto configuration programming assigns phones and directory numbers in a first-come-first-served sequential manner.

Installing IP Communicator

Double-click the **CiscoIPCommunicatorSetup.exe** icon (or run the program CiscoIPCommunicatorSetup.exe) to start the install wizard on your personal computer, as shown in Figure 2-2. Click **Next** and follow the onscreen instructions to accept the License Agreement, shown in Figure 2-3.

Figure 2-2 Cisco IP Communicator InstallShield Wizard

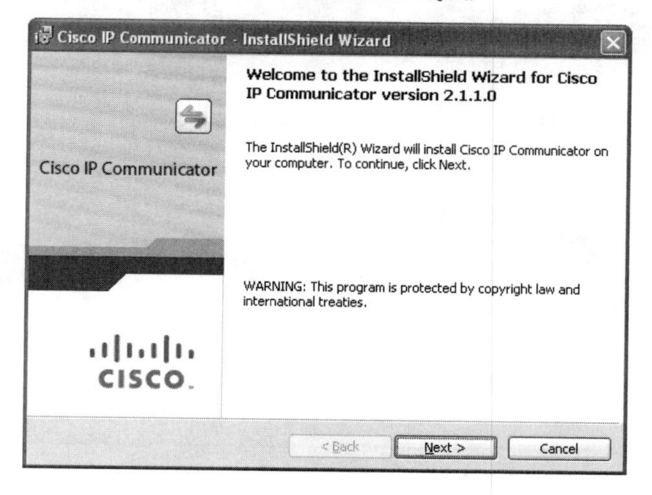

Figure 2-3 End User License Agreement

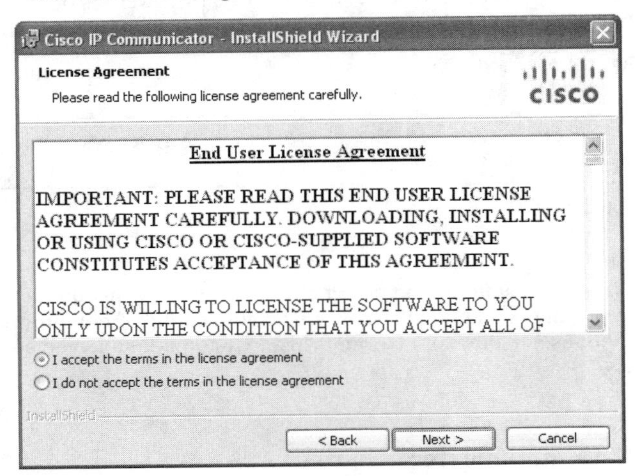

When the installation is complete, you should see the InstallShield Wizard Completed screen, as shown in Figure 2-4. Check the **Launch Cisco IP Communicator** check box and click **Finish**. The Audio Tuning Wizard screen appears.

Figure 2-4 InstallShield Wizard Completed

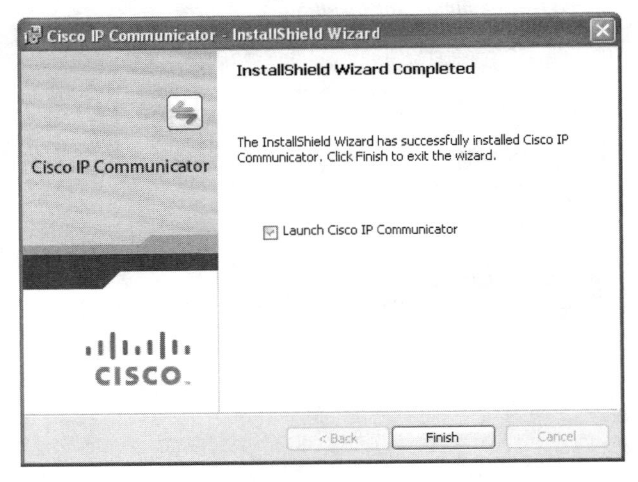

Figure 2-5 shows the select audio devices screen of the Audio Tuning Wizard. Follow the instructions and then click **Next** to continue.

Figure 2-5 Audio Tuning Wizard

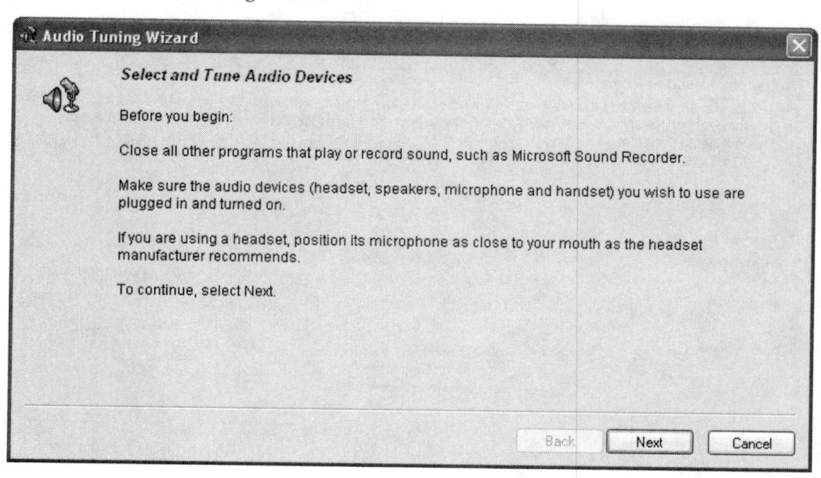

On the next screen, shown in Figure 2-6, you choose the appropriate devices from the drop-down lists and click **Next**.

Figure 2-6 Select Audio Devices

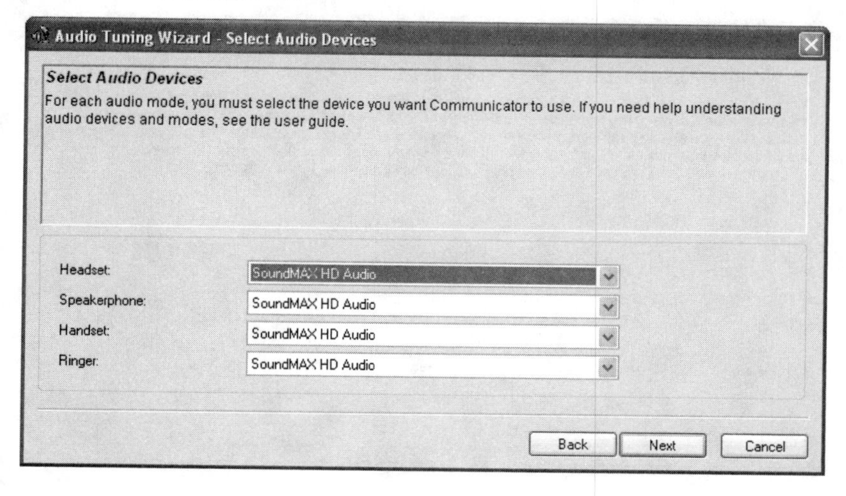

Figure 2-7 shows the Adjust the Listening Volume screen. Click **Play** and follow the onscreen instructions to adjust the listening volume. Click **Next** to continue.

Figure 2-7 Adjust the Listening Volume

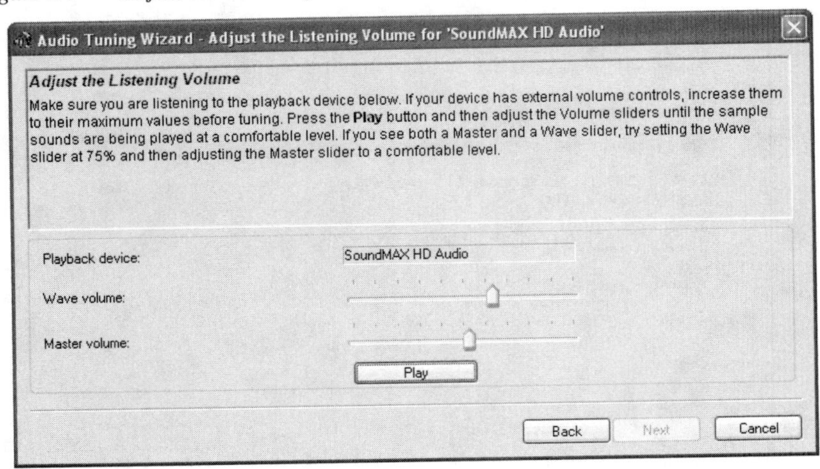

Figure 2-8 shows the Adjust the Microphone Volume screen. Click the **Test** button and follow the onscreen instructions to adjust the microphone volume, and then click **Next**.

Figure 2-8 Adjust the Microphone Volume

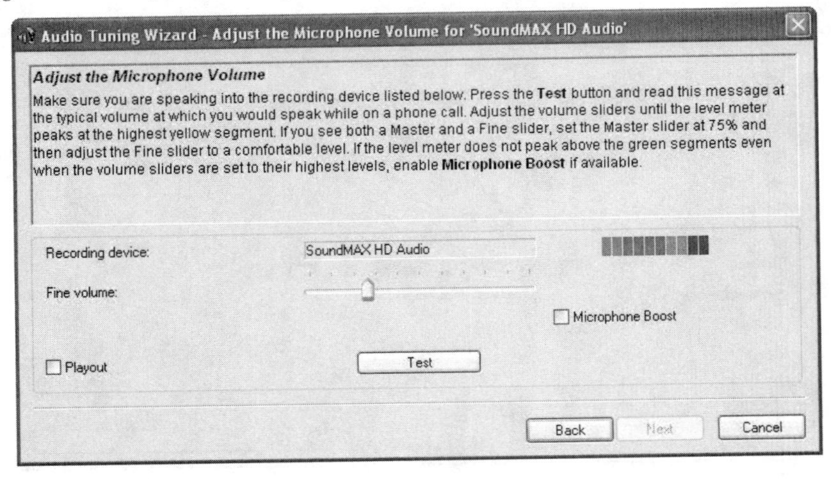

After this you will have completed the Audio Tuning Wizard. The final screen now appears, as shown in Figure 2-9.

Figure 2-9 Complete the Audio Tuning Wizard

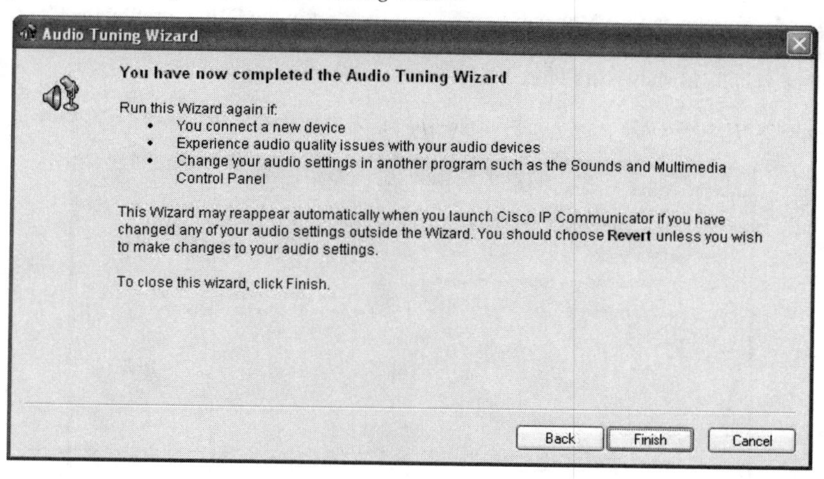

Click **Finish** to close the wizard and open the Preferences window. The Preferences window is shown in Figure 2-10.

Figure 2-10 Preferences Window

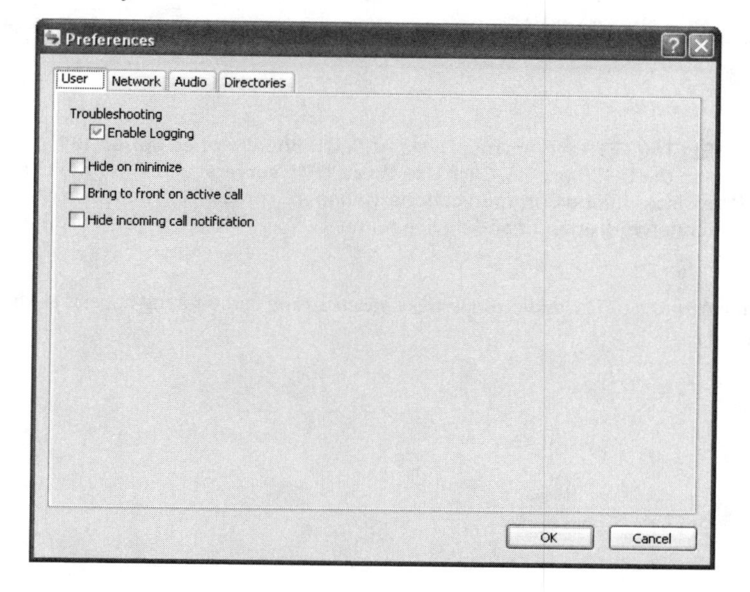

In the Preferences window, click the **Network** tab. If **option 150** pointing to the Cisco Unified Communications Manager Express has been set in the DHCP profile, the **Use the default TFTP servers** radio button will already be selected and the IP of the TFTP server(s) will be visible, as shown in Figure 2-11.

Figure 2-11 Network Preferences – Use the Default TFTP Servers

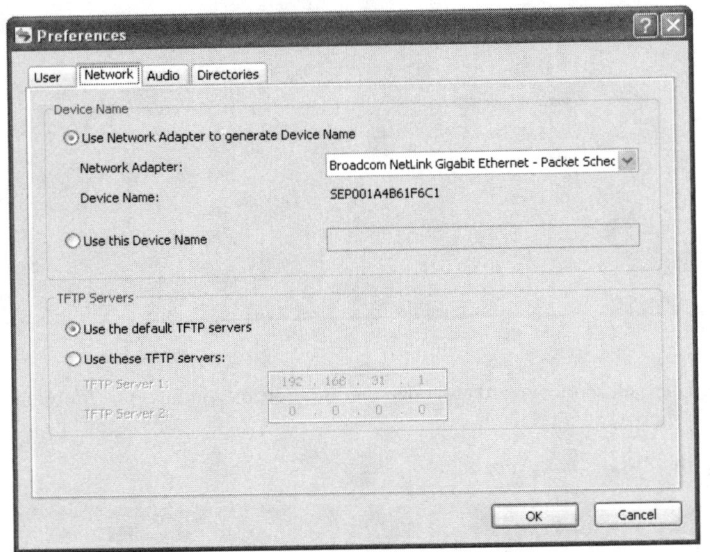

NOTE: The TFTP servers must be specified manually when **option 150** *ip-address* is not in the DHCP profile. Click **Use these TFTP servers:** and enter the IP address of the Cisco Unified Communications Manager Express. You must also choose the correct network adapter and device name.

Click the **Audio** tab. The audio properties chosen during audio tuning appear, as shown in Figure 2-12.

Figure 2-12 Audio Preferences

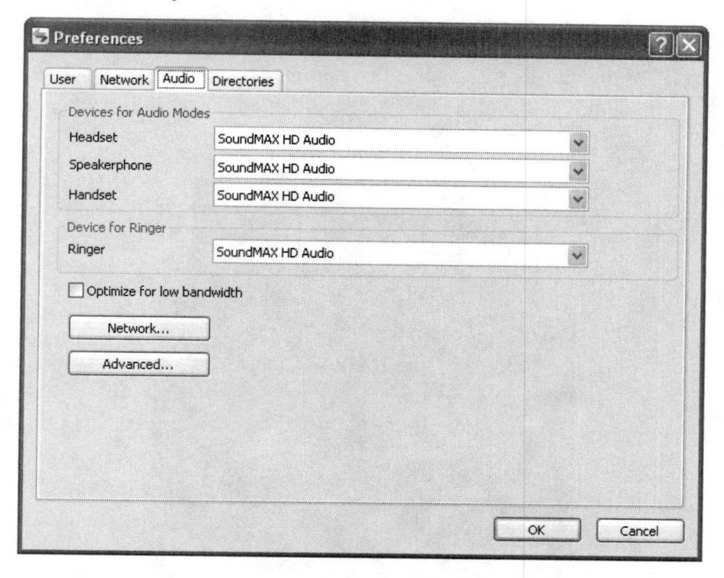

Click the **Directories** tab, as shown in Figure 2-13. Enter the Cisco Unified Communications Manager Express administrator username and password.

Figure 2-13 Directories Preferences

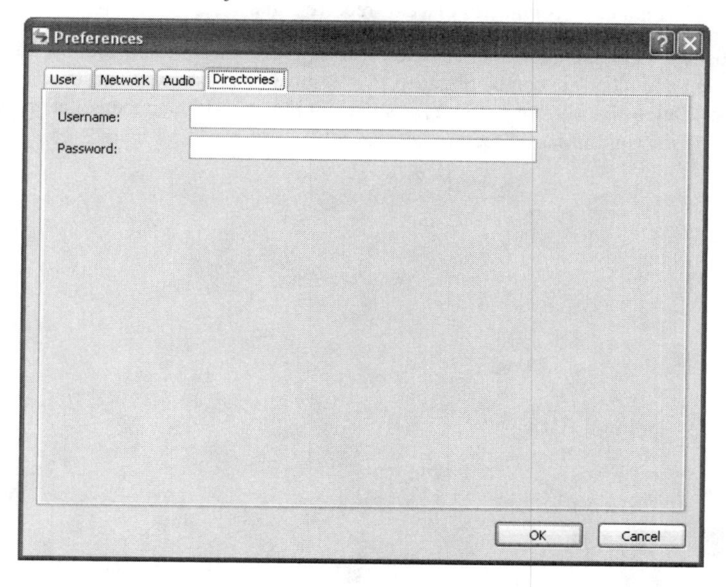

Click **OK**. Cisco IP Communicator now registers with CME.

NOTE: The initial registration with CME can take as long as a few minutes.

Open Cisco IP Communicator. An application appears, as shown in Figure 2-14.

Figure 2-14 Cisco IP Communicator

Cisco IP Communicator is ready to place or receive calls.

Call statistics, including codec, sender and receiver packet information, and the number of packets sent and received, can be obtained. A call must be in progress to view the call statistics. To view the call stats, click **?,** as shown in Figure 2-15, and then click the far end call termination (in this case directory number 5001), as shown in Figure 2-16.

Figure 2-15 Call in Progress Between 5001 and 5002

Figure 2-16 Choosing the Appropriate Connection to See the Call Statistics

Figure 2-17 shows the call statistics of the current call. Call statistics include sender and receiver codecs, sound bite size, jitter, and any lost packets.

Figure 2-17 Call Statistics

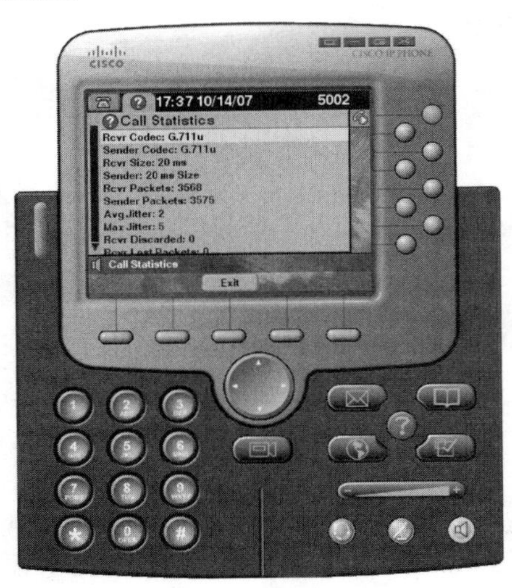

Changing Codecs Using the CLI

If you want to change codecs, enter the following commands using the CLI:

`Router(config)#` **`ephone 1`**	Enters the ephone 1 configuration mode.
`Router(config-ephone)#` **`codec g729r8`**	Specifies the G.729 codec for ephone 1.
`Router(config-ephone)#` **`ephone 2`**	Enters the ephone 2 configuration mode.
`Router(config-ephone)#` **`codec g729r8`**	Specifies the G.729 codec for ephone 2.
`Router(config-ephone)#` **`end`**	Returns to the CLI privilege exec program mode.

NOTE: The codec configuration on both ephones must be the same.

NOTE: The G.729 codec uses 29.6 kbps of bandwidth per voice stream when including the layer 2 and layer 3 overhead with the voice payload. In comparison, the G.711 codec uses 85.6 kbps of bandwidth under the same conditions.

Figure 2-18 shows the call statistics on the IP Communicator after the codec has been changed.

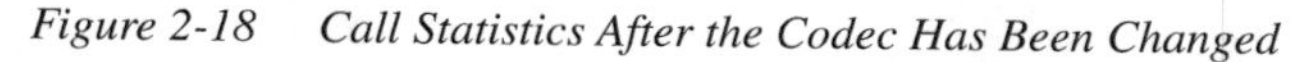

Figure 2-18 Call Statistics After the Codec Has Been Changed

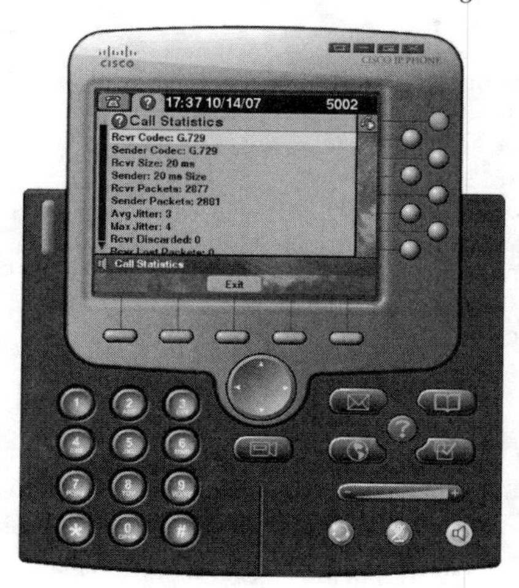

Router Configuration

Using Figure 2-1 as a reference, the following shows the output of the **show running-config** and the output of the **show flash:** commands for the router in that diagram, which detail the configuration of CME.

```
Router# show running-config
!
version 12.4
!
hostname Router
!
clock timezone CST -6
clock summer-time CST recurring 2 Sun Mar 2:00 1 Sun Nov 2:00
!
ip dhcp pool ITS
   import all
   network 192.168.30.0 255.255.255.0
   option 150 ip 192.168.31.1
   default-router 192.168.30.1
!
!
username roth privilege 15 secret 5  $some_passwordstring_this_long
!
!
interface Loopback0
 ip address 192.168.31.1 255.255.255.0
```

```
!
interface FastEthernet0/0
 ip address dhcp
 ip nat outside
!
interface FastEthernet1/0
 ip address 192.168.30.1 255.255.255.0
 ip nat inside
!
ip route 0.0.0.0 0.0.0.0 FastEthernet0/0
!
ip nat inside source list 1 interface FastEthernet0/0 overload
!
access-list 23 permit 192.168.30.0 0.0.0.255
tftp-server flash:P00308000400.bin
!
!
telephony-service
 load 7960-7940 P00308000400
 max-ephones 8
 max-dn 4
 ip source-address 192.168.31.1 port 2000
 auto assign 1 to 4
max-conferences 4 gain -6
 moh music-on-hold.au
 transfer-system full-consult
 create cnf-files version-stamp 7960 Oct 09 2007 19:17:26
!
!
ephone-dn  1  dual-line
 number 5001
!
ephone-dn  2  dual-line
 number 5002
!
ephone-dn  3  dual-line
 number 5003
!
ephone-dn  4  dual-line
 number 5004
!
!
ephone  1
 no multicast-moh
 mac-address 0050.DA7C.AB03
 codec g729r8
 type CIPC
 button  1:1
!
ephone  2
```

```
 no multicast-moh
 mac-address 001A.4B61.F6C1
 codec g729r8
 type CIPC
 button  1:2
!
ephone  3
 no multicast-moh
!
ephone  4
 no multicast-moh
!
!
banner login #

   User Authentication Required

#
!
line con 0
 login local
line aux 0
 login local
line vty 0 4
 access-class 23 in
 login local
 transport input telnet
!
ntp clock-period 17208155
ntp server <IP of time server> source FastEthernet0/0 prefer
end

Router# show flash:

System flash directory:
File  Length   Name/status
  1   21086616  c1700-ipvoicek9-mz.124-15.T1.bin
  2   4627     admin_user.html
  3   653758   admin_user.js
  4   1029     CiscoLogo.gif
  5   618      CME_GUI_README.TXT
  6   953      Delete.gif
  7   16344    dom.js
  8   864      downarrow.gif
  9   6146     ephone_admin.html
 10   4658     logohome.gif
 11   3724     normal_user.html
 12   80033    normal_user.js
 13   1347     Plus.gif
 14   843      sxiconad.gif
```

```
 15   174       Tab.gif
 16   2410      telephony_service.html
 17   870       uparrow.gif
 18   9968      xml-test.html
 19   3412      xml.template
 20   129828    P00308000400.bin
 21   461       P00308000400.loads
 22   701768    P00308000400.sb2
 23   130232    P00308000400.sbn
 24   496521    music-on-hold.au
[23338772 bytes used, 9953512 available, 33292284 total]
32768K bytes of processor board System flash (Read/Write)
```

CHAPTER 3

Introduction to IP QoS

This chapter provides information and commands concerning the following topics:

- Configuring QoS Through the Command-Line Interface (CLI)
- Using Modular QoS CLI (MQC) for Implementing QoS
  — Verifying QoS Classes and Policies Created with MQC
- Implementing QoS Using AutoQoS
- Implementing QoS with Cisco Security Device Manager (SDM) QoS Wizard
  — Monitoring QoS Status with Cisco SDM

Configuring QoS Through the Command-Line Interface (CLI)

NOTE: Cisco does not recommend the legacy CLI method for initially implementing QoS policies, due to time restraints and the greater likelihood of errors. It can be used to augment and fine-tune the Cisco AutoQoS method. The recommendation is to use one of the other methods described in this chapter to implement QoS.

The guidelines for using the CLI configuration method are as follows:

STEP 1. Build a traffic policy, including:

- Identify the traffic patterns
  - Classify the traffic
  - Prioritize the traffic
  - Select a proper QoS mechanism:
    — Queuing
    — Compression

STEP 2. Apply the policy to the interface

Using Modular QoS CLI (MQC) for Implementing QoS

NOTE: Cisco introduced MQC to help overcome the shortcomings of using the legacy CLI, and to utilize newer QoS tools and features available in Cisco IOS. MQC provides a building-block approach to applying QoS in that a single module can be used repeatedly to apply a policy to multiple interfaces.

The guidelines for using the MQC method are as follows:

STEP 1. Define traffic classes using the **class-map** command.

STEP 2. Define policies for the defined traffic classes using the **policy-map** command.

STEP 3. Apply the defined policies in the inbound or outbound direction to each interface, subinterface, or circuit using the **service-policy** command.

Step 1: Defining Traffic Classes Using the **class-map** Command

`Router(config)# class-map match-any business-traffic`	Creates a class map named "business-traffic." Of the following listed **match** statements, any of them must be matched in order to classify the traffic.
`Router(config-cmap)# match protocol ftp`	Any traffic using the FTP protocol will be classified as "business-traffic."
`Router(config-cmap)# match protocol citrix`	Any Citrix traffic will be classified as "business-traffic."
`Router(config-cmap)# exit`	Returns to global configuration mode.
`Router(config)# class-map VOIP`	Creates a class map named "VOIP."
`Router(config-cmap)# match access-group 100`	Any traffic matching access list 100 is classified as "VOIP."
`Router(config-cmap)# exit`	Returns to global configuration mode.

NOTE: Names used in the **class-map** command are case sensitive.

NOTE: If you use the **match-any** argument in the **class-map** command, only one of the listed **match** statements must be met for classification to occur. If you use the **match-all** argument, all the listed **match** statements must be met for classification to occur. If you do not use either argument, then the **match-all** argument is applied by default.

TIP: The opposite of the **match** condition is the **match not** condition.

Step 2: Defining Policies for the Traffic Classes Using the **policy-map** Command

<table>
<tr><td colspan="2">Router(config)# policy-map MYQOS-POLICY</td><td>Creates a policy map named “MYQOS-POLICY.”</td></tr>
<tr><td colspan="2">Router(config-pmap)# class VOIP</td><td>Associates the class map named “VOIP” to this policy map.</td></tr>
<tr><td rowspan="3">Choose one of these two:</td><td>Router(config-pmap-c)# priority 256</td><td>Traffic classified as “VOIP” is assigned to a priority queue that has a bandwidth guarantee of 256 Kbps.</td></tr>
<tr><td colspan="2">OR</td></tr>
<tr><td>Router(config-pmap-c)# priority percent 25</td><td>Traffic classified as “VOIP” is assigned to a priority queue that has a bandwidth guarantee of 25 percent of total available bandwidth.</td></tr>
<tr><td colspan="2">Router(config-pmap-c)# exit</td><td>Returns to config-pmap mode.</td></tr>
<tr><td colspan="2">Router(config-pmap)# class BUSINESS-TRAFFIC</td><td>Associates the class map named “BUSINESS-TRAFFIC” to this policy map.</td></tr>
<tr><td rowspan="5">Choose one of these three:</td><td>Router(config-pmap-c)# bandwidth 1000</td><td>Traffic classified as “BUSINESS-TRAFFIC” is assigned to a WFQ with a bandwidth guarantee of 1000 Kbps.</td></tr>
<tr><td colspan="2">OR</td></tr>
<tr><td>Router(config-pmap-c)# bandwidth percent 25</td><td>Traffic classified as “BUSINESS-TRAFFIC” is assigned to a WFQ with a bandwidth guarantee of 25 percent of total available bandwidth.</td></tr>
<tr><td colspan="2">OR</td></tr>
<tr><td>Router(config-pmap-c)# bandwidth remaining 25</td><td>Traffic classified as “business-traffic” is assigned to a WFQ with a bandwidth guarantee of 25 percent of the remaining bandwidth.</td></tr>
<tr><td colspan="2">Router(config-pmap-c)# exit</td><td>Returns to config-pmap mode.</td></tr>
</table>

Router(config-pmap)# **class class-default**	Associates the class map named "class-default" to this policy map. The "class-default" class map is a predefined map defined by Cisco IOS.
Router(config-pmap-c)# **fair-queue**	Traffic classified as "class-default" will be assigned to a queue that gets the rest of the available bandwidth.
Router(config-pmap-c)# **exit**	Returns to config-pmap mode.
Router(config-pmap)# **exit**	Returns to global configuration mode.

NOTE: Names used in the **policy-map** command are case sensitive.

NOTE: Up to 256 traffic classes (each defined by a class map) can be associated with a single traffic policy.

NOTE: If, within a policy map, you do not refer to the **class-default** class, any traffic that is not matched to a defined class will still be treated as **class-default**. The **class-default** will get no QoS guarantees and can have either a FIFO or a WFQ policy assigned to it.

Step 3: Applying the Defined Policies Using the **service-policy** Command

NOTE: A policy map can be applied to an interface, subinterface, virtual template, or circuit.

Router(config)# **interface serial 0/0/0**	Moves to interface configuration mode.
Router(config-if)# **service-policy output MYQOS-POLICY**	Assigns the policy named "MYQOS-POLICY" to this interface in an outbound direction.
	A policy map can be set in either direction, inbound or outbound, using the keywords **input** or **output**.

NOTE: You can apply a defined and configured policy map to more than one interface.

TIP: Multiple policy maps can be nested to influence the sequence of QoS actions.

TIP: It is recommended to reuse class maps and policy maps because this promotes standardization and helps to reduce the chance of errors.

Verifying QoS Classes and Policies Created with MQC

Command	Description
`Router# show class-map`	Displays all configured class maps.
`Router# show policy-map`	Displays all configured policy maps.
`Router# show policy-map interface serial 0/0/0`	Displays the policy map that is applied to the serial 0/0/0 interface. Also shows QoS interface statistics.

Configuration Example: Enforcing a Sub-Rate

A sub-rate is a virtual pipe that is a smaller amount than the physical capacity of a larger pipe. In this example, you need to enforce a sub-rate (that is, a 10-Mbps virtual pipe on a 1-Gbps link) on a particular link, while offering minimum bandwidth guarantees to applications such as voice, mission-critical applications, and video within that virtual pipe as follows:

- Voice: 1 Mbps
- Mission-critical applications traffic: 2 Mbps
- Video: 5 Mbps
- Remaining bandwidth allocated to best-effort traffic within the defined 10-Mbps pipe

The following configuration will show the policy maps that can be created to enforce this. A policy map defines a traffic policy, which configures the QoS features associated with a traffic class that was previously identified using a class map. Class maps classifying the traffic are assumed to have already been created based on parameters not given here—protocol type, port number, ACL, and so on. Multiple policy maps can be nested to influence the sequence of QoS actions. In this example, the policy map named "CHILD" will be nested within a second policy map called "PARENT" in order to ensure that the policies of "CHILD" are enforced first.

Router(config)# **policy-map CHILD**	Creates a policy map named "CHILD."
Router(config-pmap)# **class VOICE**	Associates the class map named "VOICE" to this policy map.
Router(config-pmap-c)# **priority 1000**	Traffic classified as "VOICE" is assigned to a priority queue that has a bandwidth guarantee of 1000 Kbps (1 Mbps).
Router(config-pmap-c)# **exit**	Returns to config-pmap mode.
Router(config-pmap)# **class MISSION_CRITICAL**	Associates the class map named "MISSION_CRITICAL" to this policy map.
Router(config-pmap-c)# **bandwidth 2000**	Traffic classified as "MISSION_CRITICAL" is assigned to a WFQ with a bandwidth guarantee of 2000 Kbps (2 Mbps).
Router(config-pmap-c)# **exit**	Returns to config-pmap mode.
Router(config-pmap)# **class VIDEO**	Associates the class map named "VIDEO" to this policy map.
Router(config-pmap-c)# **bandwidth 5000**	Traffic classified as "VIDEO" is assigned to a WFQ with a bandwidth guarantee of 5000 Kbps (5 Mbps).
Router(config-pmap-c)# **exit**	Returns to config-pmap mode.
Router(config-pmap)# **exit**	Returns to global configuration mode.
Router(config)# **policy-map PARENT**	Creates a policy map named "PARENT."
Router(config-pmap)# **class class-default**	Associates the class map named "class-default" to this policy map.
Router(config-pmap-c)# **shape average 10000000**	Specifies the average rate of shaping to be 10,000,000 bps (10 Mbps).
Router(config-pmap-c)# **service-policy CHILD**	Assigns the policy map named "CHILD" to this policy map; the parameters of CHILD will be followed first, and the parameters of PARENT will be followed second.
Router(config-pmap-c)# **exit**	Returns to config-pmap mode.
Router(config-pmap)# **exit**	Returns to global configuration mode.

Implementing QoS Using AutoQoS

The main advantage of using AutoQoS is that it simplifies the QoS configuration. If you lack the in-depth knowledge of QoS commands, AutoQoS can be used to implement QoS features consistently and accurately. After using AutoQoS, you can modify the configuration by using the MQC.

NOTE: AutoQoS was first introduced in IOS 12.2(15)T.

Before you enable AutoQoS on an interface, the following must be completed:

- Cisco Express Forwarding (CEF) should be enabled. CEF is a prerequisite for Network-Based Application Recognition (NBAR).
- NBAR should be enabled. AutoQoS for the Enterprise uses NBAR for traffic discovery and classification. AutoQoS VoIP does not.
- The correct bandwidth on the interface should be configured. AutoQoS will configure Low Latency Queueing (LLQ), Compressed Real-Time Protocol (cRTP), and Link Fragmentation and Interleaving (LFI) based on interface type and bandwidth.
  - — Ethernet interfaces have a bandwidth that is auto-sensed.
  - — Serial links will use the default bandwidth of 1544 Kbps unless bandwidth is configured.

`Router(config)# ip cef`	Enables CEF on the router.
`Router(config)# interface serial 0/0/0`	Moves to interface configuration mode.
`Router(config-if)# bandwidth 512`	Sets bandwidth to 512 Kbps for accounting and cost calculation purposes.
`Router(config-if)# ip address 192.168.1.1 255.255.255.252`	Assigns IP address and netmask to interface.
`Router(config-if)# auto qos voip`	Enables AutoQoS VoIP on this interface.

NOTE: The command **auto qos voip** is from the first generation of AutoQoS. This command is used to automate the generation of QoS commands to prepare the device for VoIP traffic. The second generation is known as "AutoQoS for the Enterprise" and the command **auto discovery qos** must first be entered so that the router will discover and analyze network traffic. This discovery and analysis is done using NBAR. After the **auto discovery qos** command is entered, the command **auto qos** must be entered. This will allow for the creation of class maps based on the results of the discovery, and finally the creation and application of policy maps on the interface.

Implementing QoS with Cisco Security Device Manager (SDM) QoS Wizard

The Cisco Security Device Manager (SDM) allows a network administrator with little experience of the Cisco IOS to easily configure routing, security, and QoS services on a Cisco router. The Cisco SDM QoS Wizard offers easy optimization of LAN, WAN, and VPN bandwidth and application for different business needs.

NOTE: Within the SDM are three predefined categories for business needs: Real Time; Business-Critical; and Best-Effort.

NOTE: The Cisco SDM QoS Wizard supports NBAR.

As shown in Figure 3-1, from the home page of SDM, click the **Configure** button at the top of the page, and then click the **Quality of Service** icon in the Tasks toolbar on the left.

Figure 3-1 Quality of Service

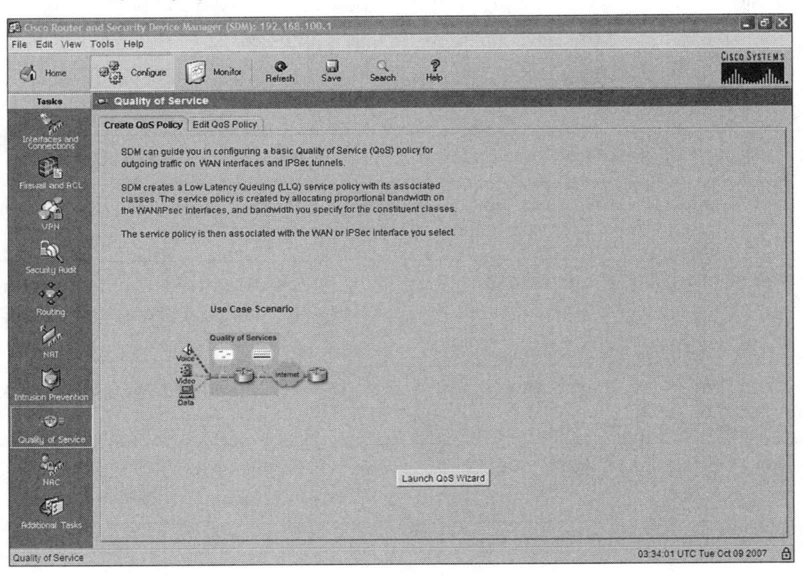

From this page you have two different tabs that you can start from: **Create QoS Policy** and **Edit QoS Policy**. Click the **Create QoS Policy** tab, and then click **Launch QoS Wizard** located in the bottom-right corner to start the QoS Wizard. The first screen of the wizard is shown in Figure 3-2.

Figure 3-2 Quality of Service Wizard

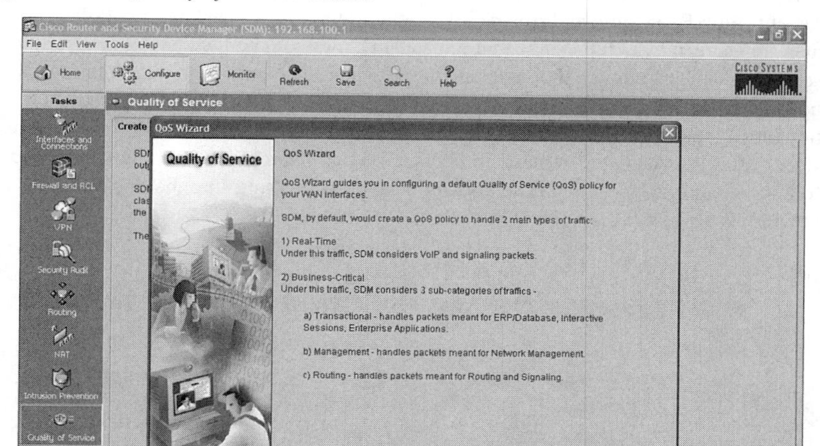

Clicking the **Next** button takes you to the second screen of the QoS Wizard: Interface Selection. Choose the interface on which this QoS policy will be applied, as shown in Figure 3-3. If you want to see specific details about an interface, you can select an interface and then click the **Details** button. Click the **Next** button to continue.

Figure 3-3 Interface Selection

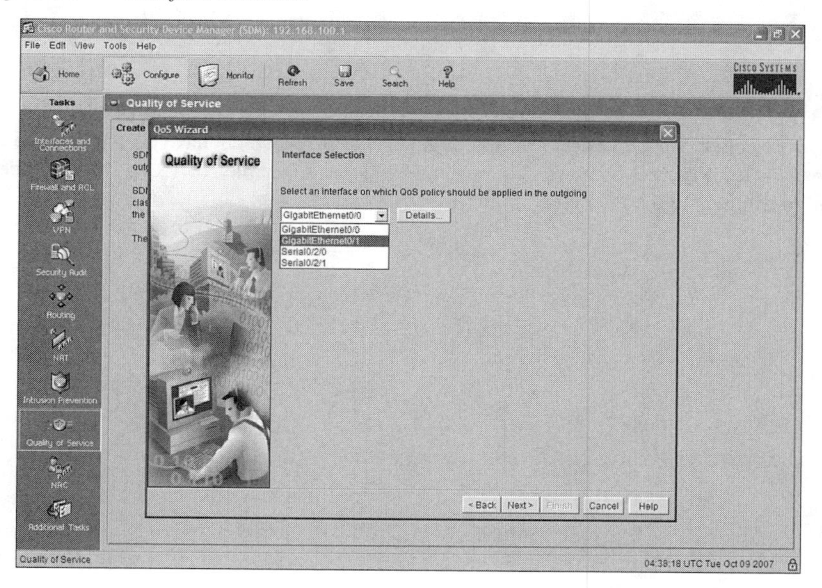

SDM will now help you create a QoS policy to provide quality of service to two different types of traffic: Real-Time and Business-Critical. Figure 3-4 shows the QoS Policy Generation screen, which prompts you to enter in bandwidth percentages for each class. Cisco SDM will not allow you to allocate more than 75 percent of the total interface bandwidth to one or more QoS classes. SDM recommends 72 percent of available bandwidth allocation for real-time traffic and 3 percent of available bandwidth for business-critical traffic. As you enter in these numbers, SDM will automatically calculate the Best-Effort class and bandwidth requirements for each class, making sure that the total bandwidth is always 100 percent. Click **Next** to continue.

Figure 3-4 QoS Policy Generation

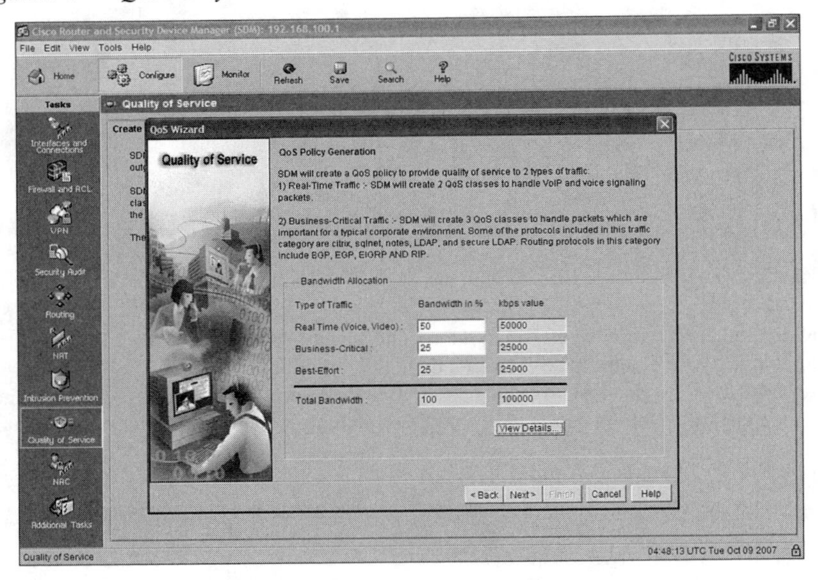

After you click **Next**, an SDM warning might appear if you do not have NBAR enabled on the interface. Figure 3-5 shows this warning. Click **Yes** to enable NBAR on the interface and to continue to the last screen of the wizard.

Figure 3-5 SDM Warning

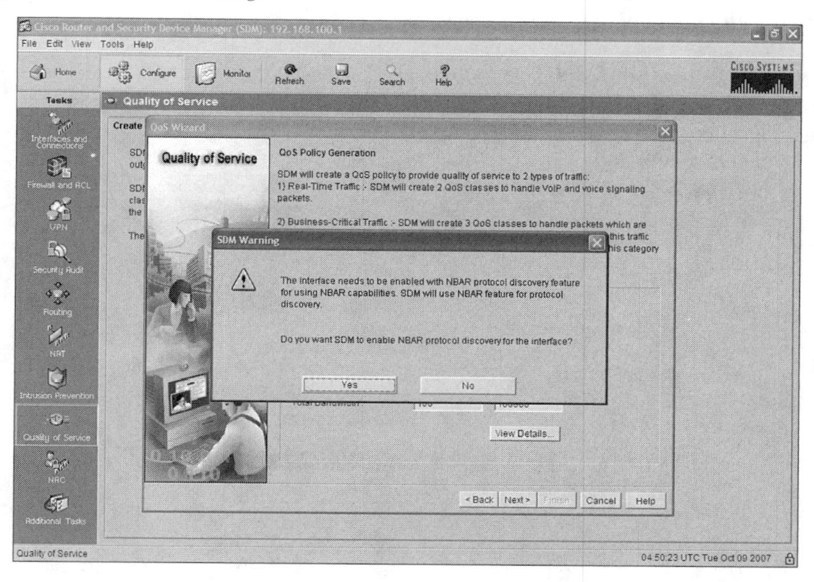

Figure 3-6 shows the final screen of the QoS Wizard, the summary of the configuration. After reviewing the configuration to ensure no errors, click **Finish** to deliver the configuration to the router.

Figure 3-6 Configuration Summary

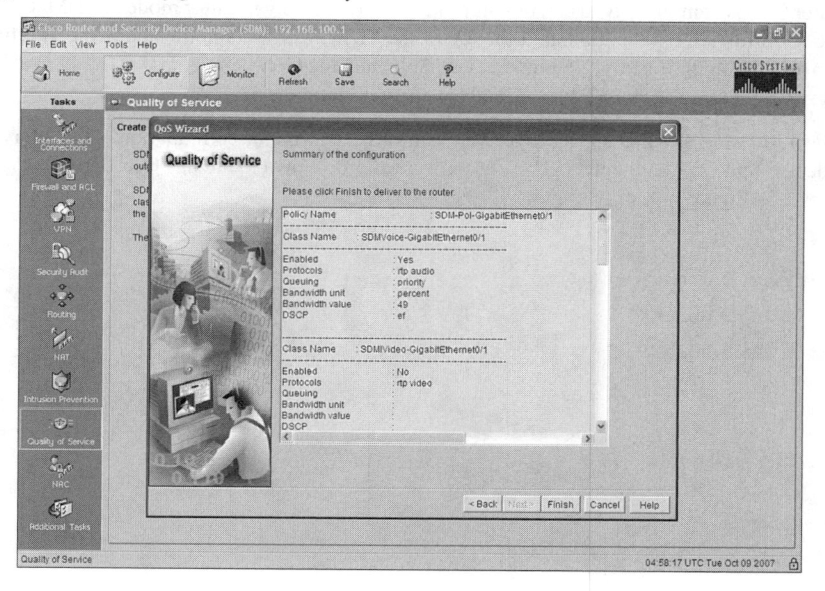

Figure 3-7 shows the Commands Delivery Status window. Click **OK** to close the window, and the **Edit QoS Policy** tab in SDM appears.

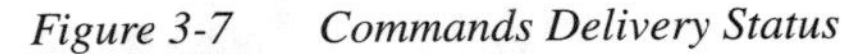

Figure 3-7 Commands Delivery Status

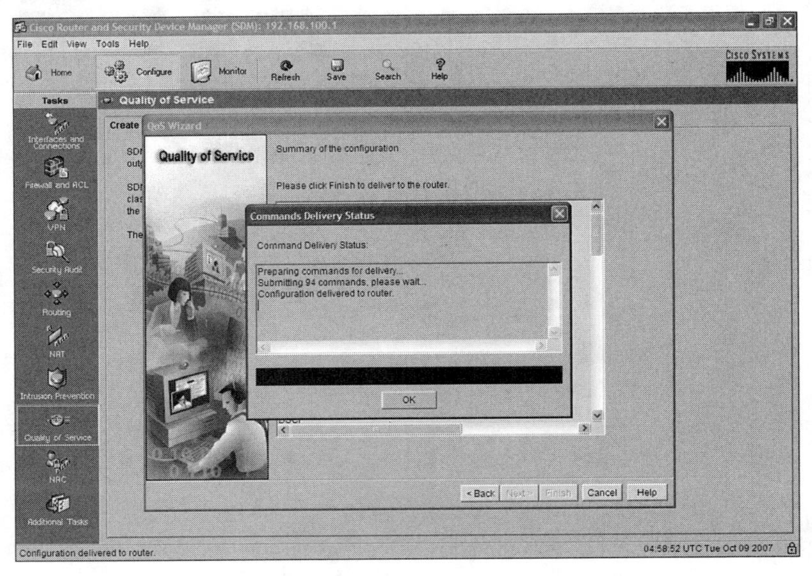

Monitoring QoS Status with Cisco SDM

After QoS is configured you can monitor its status by entering monitor mode in SDM. Click the **Monitor** icon in the toolbar at the top of the SDM window, and then click the **Traffic Status** icon in the Tasks toolbar on the left. Selecting the **QoS** item from the **Top N Traffic Flows** folder as shown in Figure 3-8 opens the QoS monitor.

The traffic statistics that appear in the bar charts are based on the combination of the interval selected and QoS parameters. The **View Interval** drop-down menu has four options, as shown in Figure 3-9:

- Now
- Every 1 minute
- Every 5 minutes
- Every 1 hour

Figure 3-8 Monitor QoS Status

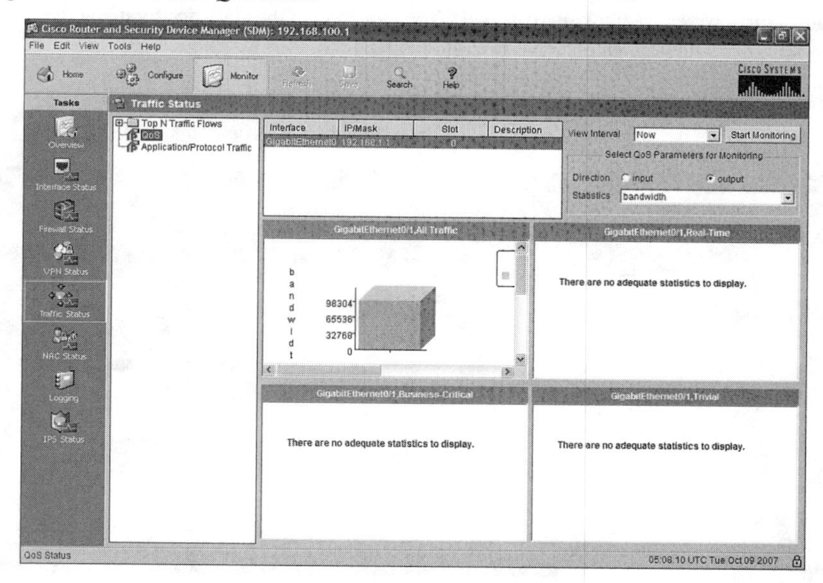

Figure 3-9 View Interval Drop-Down Menu

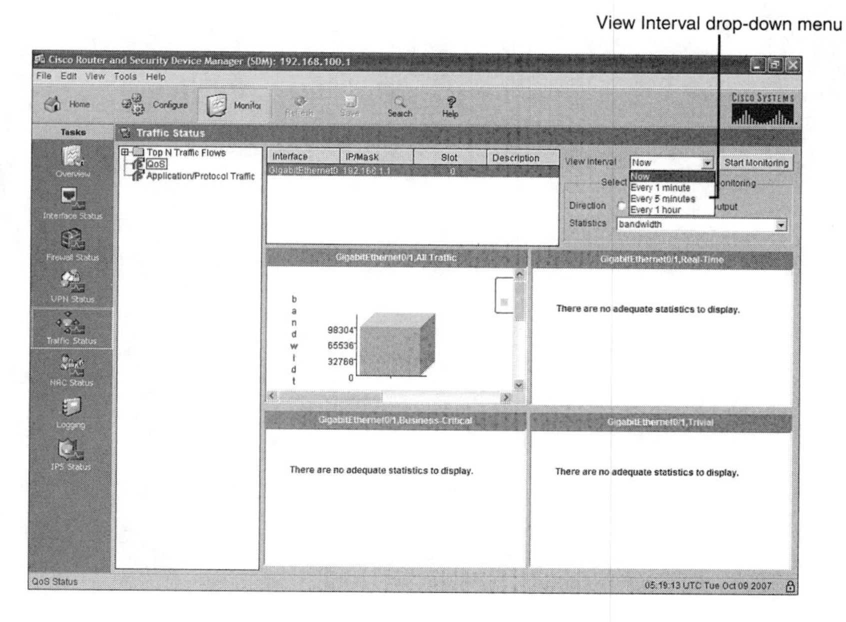

Other QoS parameters include direction of traffic flow (**input** or **output**) and statistics (**bandwidth**, **bytes**, or **packets dropped**). You can change the statistics by using the **Statistics** drop-down menu, shown in Figure 3-10.

Figure 3-10 Statistics Drop-Down Menu

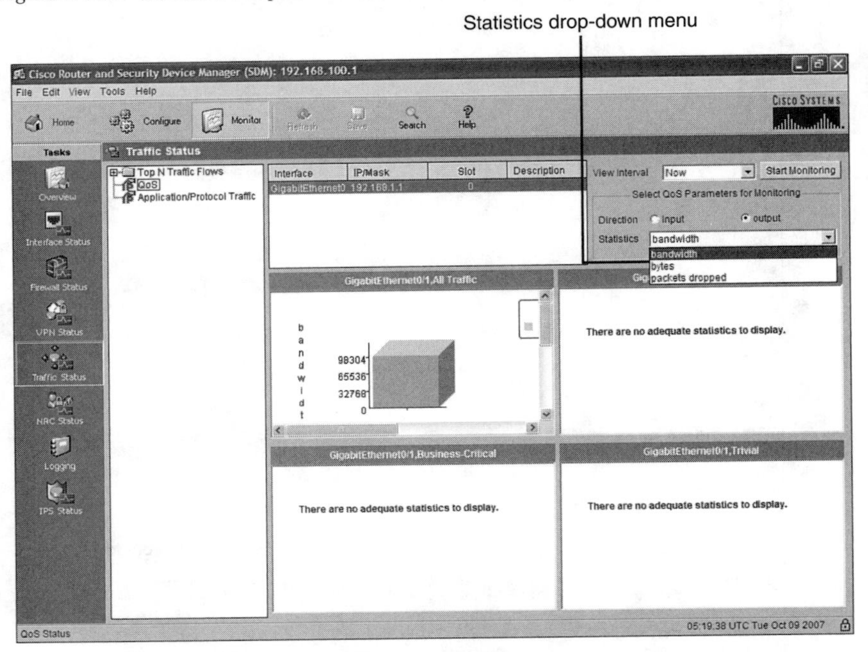

CHAPTER 4

Implementing DiffServ

This chapter provides information and commands concerning the following topics:

- Networked-Based Application Recognition (NBAR) for Classification
- Classification and Marking
- Configuring Priority Queuing (PQ)
- Configuring Custom Queuing (CQ)
- Configuring PQ & CQ for Frame Relay
- Configuring Weighted Fair Queuing (WFQ)
- Configuring Class-Based Weighted Fair Queuing (CBWFQ)
- Configuring Low-Latency Queuing (LLQ)
- Configuring Low-Latency Queuing (LLQ) with Class-Based Weighted Random Early Detection (CBWRED)
- Traffic Policing
  - — Single Token Bucket/Single Rate
  - — Two Token Bucket/Two Rate
- Traffic Shaping
  - — Per-Interface Traffic Shaping
  - — Class-Based Traffic Shaping
- Implementing QoS Preclassify

Networked-Based Application Recognition (NBAR) for Classification

Command	Description
Router(config)# **interface fastethernet 0/0**	Moves to interface configuration mode.
Router(config)# **ip nbar protocol-discovery**	Turns on NBAR protocol discovery at the interface.
Router(config)# **exit**	Returns to privileged mode.

<table>
<tr><td><pre>Router# show ip nbar port-map protocol-name</pre></td><td>Displays the TCP/UDP port number(s) used by NBAR to classify a given protocol.</td></tr>
<tr><td><pre>Router# show ip nbar protocol-discovery

 FastEthernet0/0
             Input   Output
             -----   ------
  Protocol   Packet Count   Packet Count
             Byte Count   Byte Count
             5min Bit Rate (bps)   5min Bit Rate (bps)
             5min Max   5min Max
             Bit Rate (bps)   Bit Rate (bps)
  ------------------------ ------------------------ ---
  h323   424   0
               295978   0
               0   0
               6000   0
  dns   3809   0
               1046342   0
               0   0
               4000   0
  http   151   0
               167355   0
               0   0
               4000   0</pre></td><td>Displays the statistics for all the interfaces on which NBAR is enabled.</td></tr>
</table>

NOTE: NBAR is the discovery mechanism for class-map "match" statements when filtering by protocol.

Classification and Marking

The tasks to classify traffic are

STEP 1. Create a class-map for each interesting traffic grouping.

STEP 2. Choose the interesting traffic.

Step 1: Create a Class-Map for Each Interesting Traffic Grouping

Router(config)# **class-map match-any MAPNAME**	Creates a class-map MAPNAME using **Logical-OR** for all matching statements.
OR	
Router(config)# **class-map match-all MAPNAME**	Creates a class-map MAPNAME using **Logical-AND** for all matching statements.

NOTE: If neither **match-all** nor **match-any** are specified in the **class-map** command, the default **match-all** is used.

Step 2: Choose the Interesting Traffic

Router(config-cmap)# **match access-group name LETWEBIN**	Selects traffic by access control list (ACL) name or number.
Router(config-cmap)# **match cos 1 2 3**	Selects traffic by one or more Layer 2 class of service (CoS) value(s).
Router(config-cmap)# **match source-address mac 00:00:00:00:00:00**	Selects traffic by source MAC address.
Router(config-cmap)# **match destination-address mac 00:00:00:00:00:00**	Selects traffic by destination Media Access Control (MAC) address.
Router(config-cmap)# **match discard-class 2**	Selects traffic marked by the **set discard-class** *value* command.
Router(config-cmap)# **match dscp 1 2 af11**	Selects traffic by one or more differentiated services code point (DSCP) value(s).
Router(config-cmap)# **match fr-de**	Selects traffic by a set discard eligible bit.
Router(config-cmap)# **match fr-dlci 416**	Selects traffic by Frame Relay data-link connection identifier (DLCI) number.
Router(config-cmap)# **match input-interface serial0/0/0**	Selects traffic by input interface name.

`Router(config-cmap)# match vlan 55-59 82`	Selects traffic in a single VLAN, a range of VLANs, or both.
`Router(config-cmap)# match qos-group 3`	Selects traffic marked by the **set qos-group** *value* command.
	NOTE: Use NBAR for classification by using the **match protocol** *protocol-name* command.
`Router(config-cmap)# match protocol bgp`	Selects traffic by NBAR protocol discovery.
`Router(config-cmap)# match class-map CLASSMAPNAME`	Selects traffic by nesting a class-map in a class-map.
	NOTE: Traffic classes can be nested within one another, saving users the overhead of re-creating a new traffic class when most of the information exists in a previously configured traffic class. In the previous example, traffic class CLASSMAPNAME could have the same characteristics of another class-map with the exception of a single line. Rather than reconfigure the class-map line for line, you can nest one class-map inside another class-map.
`Router(config-cmap)# exit`	Exit class-map configuration mode.

The tasks to mark traffic are

STEP 3. Create a policy.

STEP 4. Choose the class of traffic.

STEP 5. Mark the traffic in the class.

STEP 6. Apply the policy to an interface.

Step 3: Create a Policy

Router(config)# **policy-map MARKINGPOLICY**	Creates the marking policy MARKINGPOLICY.

Step 4: Choose the Class of Traffic

Router(config-pmap)# **class MAPNAME**	Chooses the class to use in this policy.

Step 5: Mark the Traffic in the Class

Router(config-pmap-c)# **set dscp af41**	Sets the DSCP of the traffic class MAPNAME to "af41".
Router(config-pmap-c)# **exit**	Exits out of config-pmac-c mode and returns to config-pmap mode.

NOTE: Repeat steps 4 and 5 until all required classes are defined.

Step 4 (repeated): Choose the Class of Traffic

Router(config-pmap)# **class CLASSMAPNAME**	Add another class of traffic to policy MARKINGPOLICY.

Step 5 (repeated): Mark the Traffic in the Class

Router(config-pmap)# **set cos 3**	Marks the packets in class MYMAPCLASS with a CoS value of 3.
Router(config-pmap-c)# **set precedence 5**	Marks the packets in class MYMAPCLASS with a precedence value of 5.
Router(config-pmap-c)# **set qos-group 4**	Sets a group identifier that is used to classify packets.
Router(config-pmap-c)# **exit**	Finishes defining the policy for class MYMAPNAME.

Step 6: Apply the Policy to an Interface

`Router(config)#` **`interface serial 0/0/0`**	Chooses which interface to set the marking policy.
`Router(config-if)#` **`service-policy output MARKINGPOLICY`**	Applies the marking policy to outbound traffic.

Configuring Priority Queuing (PQ)

Figure 4-1 shows a flowchart for the configuration that follows, which shows how to configure priority queuing.

Figure 4-1 Priority Queuing

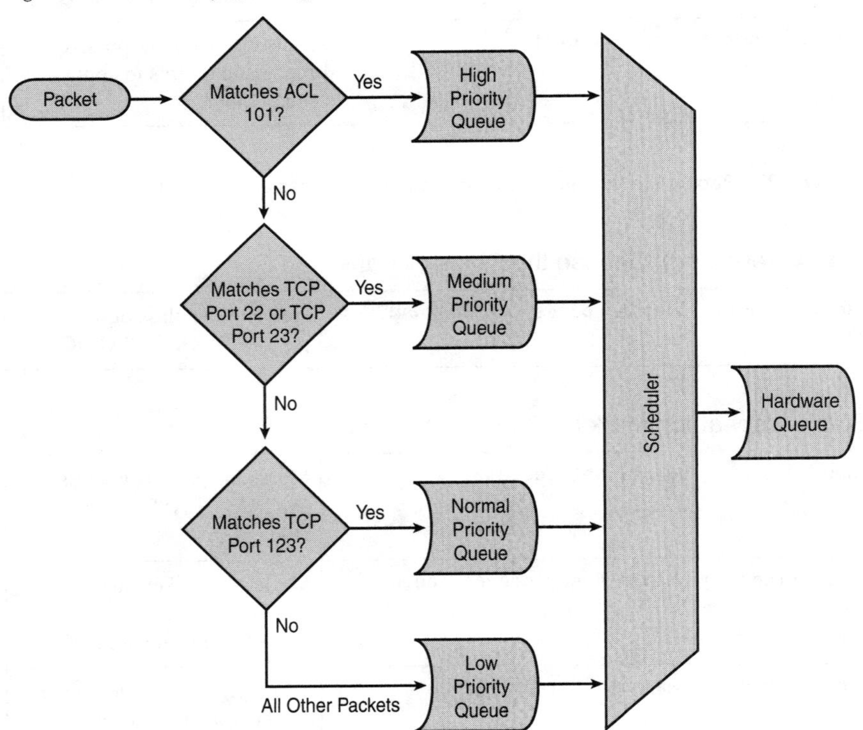

Priority queuing is configured using these steps:

STEP 1. Globally define the classification methods.

STEP 2. Assign traffic for individual queues.

STEP 3. Optionally establish the packet limit for each queue.

STEP 4. Apply the priority queuing list to an interface.

STEP 5. Verify your configuration.

Step 1: Globally Define the Classification Methods

`Router(config)#` **`access-list 101 permit ip any any precedence internet`**	Creates an ACL to define interesting traffic.

Step 2: Assign Traffic for Individual Queues

`Router(config)#` **`priority-list 5 protocol ip high list 101`**	Assigns access list 101 to specify traffic to the "high" priority queue.
`Router(config)#` **`priority-list 5 protocol ip medium tcp 22`**	Assigns TCP port 22 traffic to the "medium" priority queue.
`Router(config)#` **`priority-list 5 protocol ip medium tcp 23`**	Assigns TCP port 23 traffic to the "medium" priority queue.
`Router(config)#` **`priority-list 5 protocol ip normal tcp 123`**	Assigns TCP port 123 traffic to the "normal" priority queue.
`Router(config)#` **`priority-list 5 default low`**	Defines a default queue for traffic not specified in another queue.

Step 3: Optionally Establish the Packet Limit for Each Queue

`Router(config)#` **`priority-list 5 queue-limit 20 40 60 100`**	Specifies the maximum number of packets for each queue.

NOTE: No packet in a priority queue is sent until all higher priority queues are empty. This can result in the starvation of the lower priority queues.

Step 4: Apply the Priority Queuing List to an Interface

`Router(config)# interface serial0/0`	Enters interface programming mode.
`Router(config-if)# priority-group 5`	Applies the priority list.

Step 5: Verify Your Configuration

`Router# show queuing`	Lists all or selected configured queuing strategies.
`Router# show queue serial 0/0/3`	Lists all queuing information on interface serial 0/0/3.
`Router# debug priority`	Displays priority queuing output.

Configuring Custom Queuing (CQ)

Figure 4-2 shows a flowchart for the configuration that follows, which shows how to configure custom queuing.

The tasks to configure custom queuing are

STEP 1. Define classification methods to select traffic for individual queues.

STEP 2. Specify the byte count and packet limit for each queue (optional).

STEP 3. Apply the custom queue to an interface.

Figure 4-2 Custom Queuing

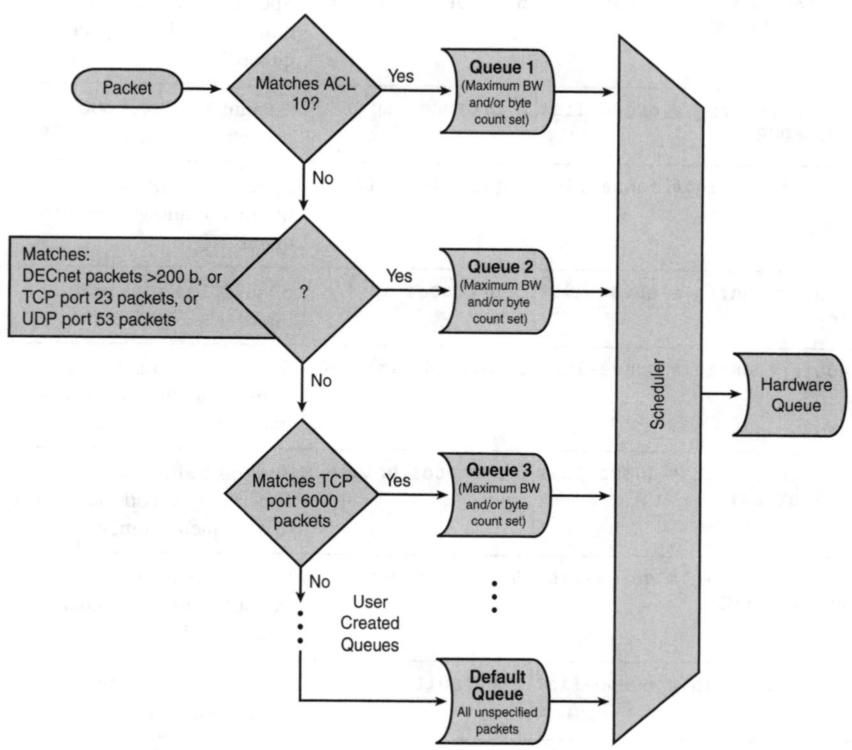

Command	Description
`Router(config)#` **`queue-list 5 protocol ip 1 list 10`**	Moves traffic that matches IP access list 10 to queue number 1.
`Router(config)#` **`queue-list 5 queue 1 limit 10`**	Specifies the maximum number allowed packets in queue 1.
`Router(config)#` **`queue-list 5 protocol decnet 2 gt 200`**	Selects DECnet packets with a size greater than 200 bytes to queue number 2.
`Router(config)#` **`queue-list 5 protocol ip 2 tcp 23`**	Assigns Telnet packets to queue number 2.
`Router(config)#` **`queue-list 5 protocol ip 2 udp 53`**	Sends User Datagram Protocol (UDP) Domain Name Service packets to queue number 2.

Router(config)# **queue-list 5 queue 2 limit 5**	Specifies the maximum number of allowed packets in queue 2.
Router(config)# **queue-list 5 protocol ip 3 udp 6000**	Assigns UDP port 6000 packets to queue number 3.
Router(config)# **queue-list 5 queue 3 limit 25**	Specifies the maximum number of allowed packets in queue 3.
Router(config)# **queue-list 5 protocol ip 4 tcp www**	Sends HTTP packets to queue 4.
Router(config)# **queue-list 5 queue 4 limit 40**	Specifies the maximum number of allowed packets in queue 4.
Router(config)# **queue-list 5 protocol bridge 5 list 201**	Assigns traffic that matches Ethernet type code access list 201 to queue number 5.
Router(config)# **queue-list 5 queue 5 byte-count 14500**	Establishes a 14,500 byte count for queue number 5 in queue list 5.
Router(config)# **queue-list 5 default 6**	Specifies queue 6 for all unspecified traffic.
Router(config)# **interface serial 0/0/0**	Moves to interface configuration mode.
Router(config-if)# **custom-queue-list 5**	Assigns custom queue-list 5 to this interface.

NOTE: Unlike a priority queue, a custom queue can control the available bandwidth and queue service byte count on an interface when unable to accommodate the aggregate traffic leaving the interface.

Configuring PQ & CQ for Frame Relay

Priority queuing for Frame Relay is configured using these steps:

STEP 1. Enable Frame Relay Traffic Shaping.

STEP 2. Select interesting traffic.

STEP 3. Create a priority list and custom queue list.

STEP 4. Create a map class to call the priority list and/or custom queue list.

STEP 5. Apply the map class to a Frame Relay interface.

Step 1: Enable Frame Relay Traffic Shaping

Router(config)# **interface serial0/0**	Moves to interface configuration mode.
Router(config-if)# **frame-relay traffic-shaping**	Configures a Frame Relay map class.

Step 2: Select Interesting Traffic

Router(config)# **access-list 10 permit ip 192.168.100.32 0.0.0.3**	Chooses source addresses for high priority handling.

Step 3: Create a Priority List and Custom Queue List

Router(config)# **priority-list 5 protocol ip high list 10**	Assigns an access list to specify traffic to the "high" priority queue.
Router(config)# **priority-list 5 protocol ip medium tcp 23**	Assigns TCP port 23 traffic to the "medium" priority queue.
Router(config)# **priority-list 5 protocol ip normal tcp 123**	Assigns TCP port 123 traffic to the "normal" priority queue.
Router(config)# **priority-list 5 default low**	Defines a default queue for traffic not specified in another queue.
Router(config)# **priority-list 5 queue-limit 20 40 60 100**	Specifies the maximum number of packets for each queue.
Router(config)# **queue-list 7 protocol ip 3 udp 6000**	Assigns UDP port 6000 packets to queue number 7.

Step 4: Create a Map Class to Call the Priority List and/or Custom Queue List

Router(config)# **map-class frame-relay PRIORITY**	Creates and names a map class.
	NOTE: A map class in Frame Relay should not be confused with a class-map.

`Router(config-map-class)#` **`frame-relay priority-group 5`**	Assigns priority list 5 programming to map class PRIORITY.
`Router(config-map-class)#` **`frame-relay custom-queue-list 7`**	Assigns custom queue list 7 programming to map class PRIORITY.
`Router(config-map-class)#` **`frame-relay bc 10000`**	Specifies committed burst size (bc); Default = 56,000 bits
`Router(config-map-class)#` **`frame-relay be 5000`**	Specifies excess burst size (Be), Default = 0 bits
`Router(config-map-class)#` **`frame-relay cir 64000`**	Specifies Committed Information Rate (CIR), Default = 56,000 bps
`Router(config-map-class)#` **`frame-relay traffic-rate 64000 96000`**	Specifies the average and peak traffic rates.
`Router(config-map-class)#` **`exit`**	Exits map class mode.

NOTE: The **frame-relay priority-group** command specifies legacy Cisco IOS priority queuing.

Step 5: Apply the Map Class to a Frame Relay Interface

`Router(config)#` **`interface serial0/0.100`**	Enters configure interface mode.
`Router(configif)#` **`framerelay interface-dlci 100`**	Assigns interface DLCI.
`Router(config-fr-dlci)#` **`class PRIORITY`**	Assigns the class to the virtual circuit (VC).

Configuring Weighted Fair Queuing (WFQ)

Figure 4-3 shows a flowchart for the configuration that follows, which shows how to configure Weighted Fair Queuing.

Figure 4-3 Weighted Fair Queuing

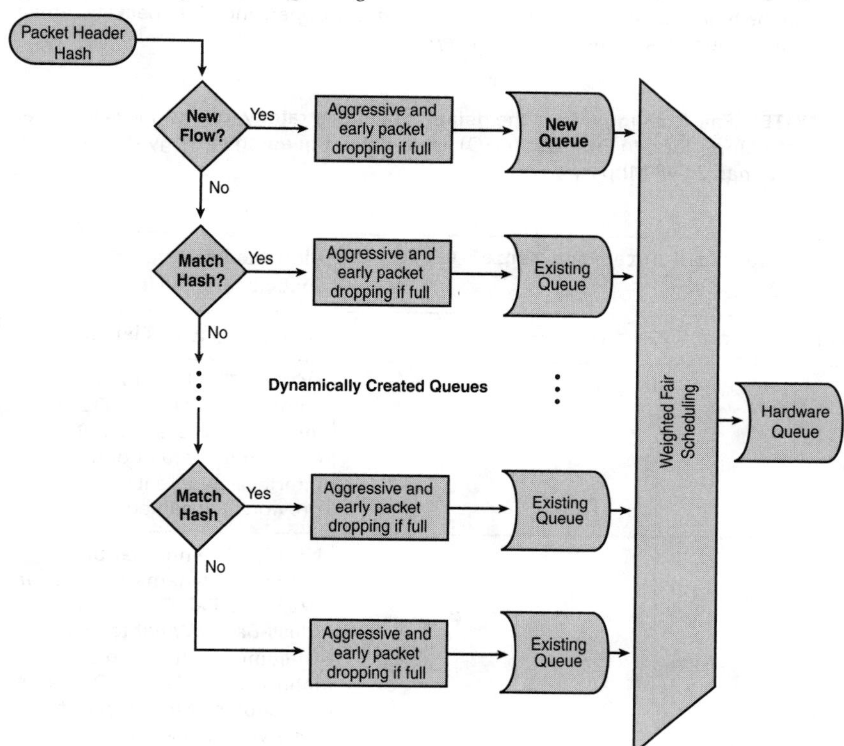

NOTE: Weighted Fair Queuing is a flow-based algorithm. Arriving packets are classified into flows, and each flow is assigned to a FIFO queue. A flow can be identified based on the following information taken from the IP header and the TCP or UDP headers:

- Source IP address
- Destination IP address
- Protocol number
- Type of Service (ToS) field
- Source TCP/UDP port number
- Destination TCP/UDP port number

These parameters are then used to generate a hash that is used as the index of the queue—if the packet is the first of a new flow, it is assigned a new queue; if the packet hash matches an existing hash, the packet is assigned to that flow queue.

NOTE: WFQ has a hold queue for all packets of all flows. If a new packet arrives and the hold queue is full, the arriving packet is dropped and older packets remain in the queue; this is known as *tail drop*.

NOTE: Fair Queuing (FQ) is the default queuing strategy for interfaces less than 2.048 Mbps. First-In-First-Out (FIFO) is the default queuing strategy for interfaces more than 2.048 Mbps.

`Router(config)# interface serial 0/0/0`	Moves to interface configuration mode.
`Router(config-if)# fair-queue`	Assigns FQ to this interface.
	NOTE: The **fair-queue** command enables WFQ on interfaces where it is not enabled by default or on interfaces where it was previously disabled.
	NOTE: The number of automatic dynamic queues for Weighted Fair Queuing and Class-Based Weighted Fair Queuing is a function of interface bandwidth. Discard thresholds, the number of reserved queues and/or dynamic queues, can be optionally specified.
`Router(config-if)# fair-queue 128 32 50`	Configures Weighted Fair Queuing with a Congestive Discard threshold of 128 packets, 32 dynamic conversation queues, and 50 reservable conversation queues.

NOTE: The congestive discard threshold must be a power of 2 in the range from 16 to 4096. The default is 64. When a conversation reaches this threshold, new message packets are discarded.

The number of dynamic queues used for best-effort conversations can be 16, 32, 64, 128, 256, 512, 1024, 2048, or 4096.

The number of reservable queues used for reserved conversations can range from 0 to 1000. The default is 0. Reservable queues are used for interfaces configured for features such as RSVP.

Configuring Class-Based Weighted Fair Queuing (CBWFQ)

Figure 4-4 shows a flowchart for the configuration that follows, which shows how to configure Class-Based Weighted Fair Queuing. Note that in the diagram, a set of bandwidths is shown to illustrate the queuing that would occur in CBWFQ. The following configuration example might show other syntax that may be used in a production environment.

Figure 4-4 Class-Based Weighted Fair Queuing

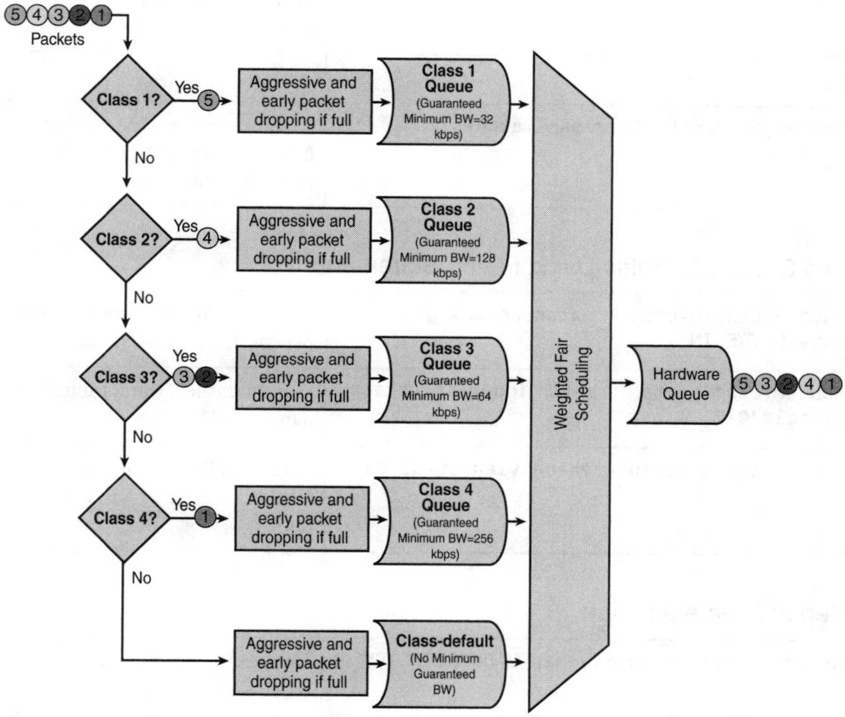

The tasks to configure Class-Based Weighted Fair Queuing are

STEP 1. Define one or more class maps.

STEP 2. Specify traffic using **match** statements.

STEP 3. Create a policy.

STEP 4. Add class maps to the policy.

STEP 5. Apply guaranteed bandwidth and maximum packet limits for each class.

STEP 6. Specify how unclassified traffic is handled.

STEP 7. Apply the policy to an interface.

STEP 8. Verify policy configuration.

Step 1: Define One or More Class Maps

Router(config)# **class-map match-any MAPNAME**	Creates class map MAPNAME using **Logical-OR** for all matching statements.
OR	
Router(config)# **class-map match-all MAPNAME**	Creates class map MAPNAME using **Logical-AND** for all matching statements.

Step 2: Specify Traffic Using Match Statements

Router(config-cmap)# **match access-group name LETWEBIN**	Selects traffic by access control list (ACL) name or number.
Router(config-cmap)# **match input-interface serial0/0/0**	Selects traffic by input interface name.
Router(config-cmap)# **match vlan 55-59 82**	Selects traffic in a single VLAN, a range of VLANs, or both.

Step 3: Create a Policy

Router(config)# policy-map **MARKINGPOLICY**	Creates the marking policy MARKINGPOLICY.

Step 4: Add Class Maps to the Policy

Router(config-pmap)# **class MAPNAME**	Specifies the interesting traffic.

Step 5: Apply Guaranteed Bandwidth and Maximum Packet Limits for Each Class

Router(config-pmap-c)# **bandwidth 128**	Sets the guaranteed bandwidth to 128 kbps.
OR	
Router(config-pmap-c)# **bandwidth percent 20**	Sets the guaranteed bandwidth to 20% of available bandwidth of the interface.
	NOTE: This number can be from 1 to 100.
	NOTE: By default, only 75% of bandwidth can be reserved. The remaining 25% is for network overhead. You can modify the default value for maximum reserved bandwidth with this interface command: Router(config-if)# **max-reserved-bandwidth 85** where **85** is the new maximum reserved bandwidth. Do not do this unless you are aware of the consequences that might occur on your network.
OR	
Router(config-pmap-c)# **bandwidth remaining percent 20**	Sets the guaranteed bandwidth to 20% of remaining bandwidth of the interface.
	NOTE: When you configure the reserved bandwidth for each traffic class in a policy map, you cannot use the **bandwidth** command on one class and the **bandwidth percent** command on another class—you must use one or the other for all classes. If you use the **percent** keyword, the sum of the percentages cannot exceed 100.

Router(config-pmap-c)# **queue-limit 55**	Specifies the maximum number of packets in the queue as 55.
Router(config-pmap-c)# **exit**	Finishes defining the policy for traffic filtered by class map MAPNAME.

Step 6: Specify How Unclassified Traffic Is Handled

Router(config-pmap)# **class class-default**	Creates a class to select the remaining traffic (not specified by any other class).
Router(config-pmap-c)# **fair-queue 16**	Specifies the number of reserved dynamic queues for unclassified traffic at 16.
Router(config-pmap-c)# **exit**	Finishes defining the policy.

Step 7: Apply the Policy to an Interface

Router(config)# **interface fastethernet 0/0**	Moves to interface configuration mode.
Router(config-if)# **service-policy output MARKINGPOLICY**	Applies the marking policy to outbound traffic.

Step 8: Verify Policy Configuration

Router# **show policy-map interface fastethernet 0/0**	Displays the configurations and statistics of policy maps applied at fastethernet 0/0.

Configuring Low-Latency Queuing (LLQ)

Figure 4-5 shows a flowchart showing the architecture of Low-Latency Queuing. The configuration that follows the diagram shows a specific example of configuring Low-Latency Queuing.

Figure 4-5 Low-Latency Queuing

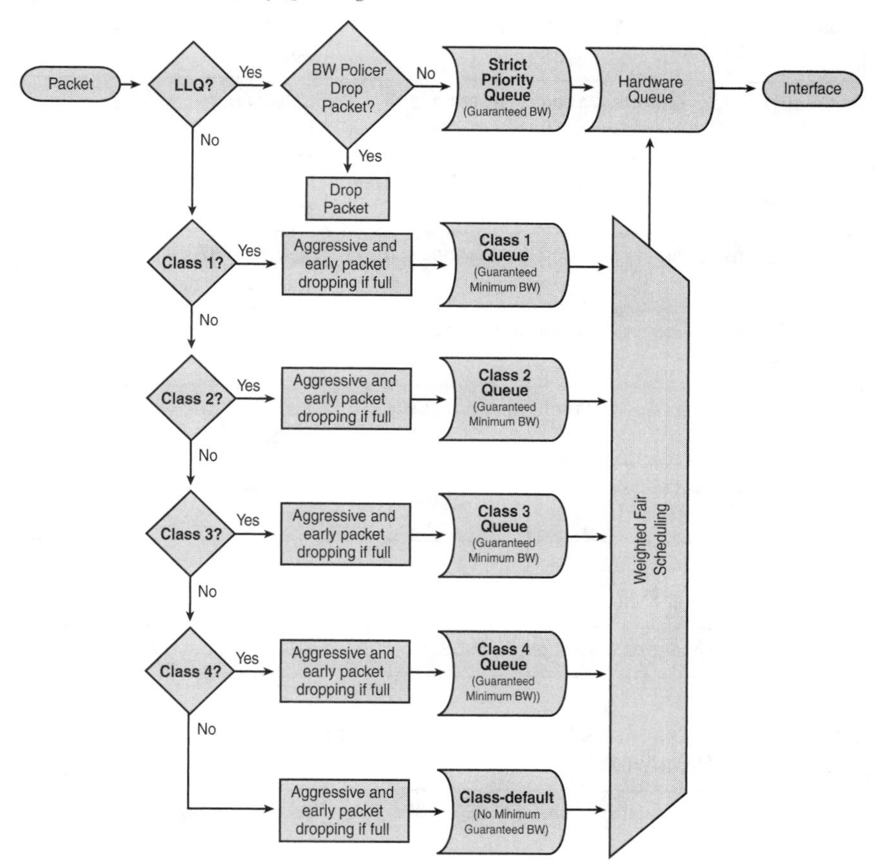

The tasks to configure Low-Latency Queuing are

STEP 1. Define one or more class maps to specify traffic.

STEP 2. Create a policy.

STEP 3. Add class maps to the policy and specify one (or more) class(es) with priority bandwidth.

STEP 4. Apply queuing policy to an interface.

STEP 5. Verify policy configuration.

Step 1: Define One or More Class Maps to Specify Traffic

Router(config-cmap)# **class-map match-any PRECEDENCE5**	Creates class for precedence 5 traffic.
Router(config-cmap)# **match precedence 5**	Selects traffic with IP precedence 5.
Router(config-cmap)# **class-map match-any PRECEDENCE7**	Creates class for precedence 7 traffic.
Router(config-cmap)# **match precedence 7**	Selects traffic with IP precedence 7.
Router(config-cmap)# **class-map match-any PRECEDENCE3**	Creates class for precedence 3 traffic.
Router(config-cmap)# **match precedence 3**	Selects traffic with IP precedence 3.
Router(config-cmap)# **class-map match-any PRECEDENCE0**	Creates class for precedence 0 traffic.
Router(config-cmap)# **match precedence 0**	Selects traffic with IP precedence 0.
Router(config-cmap)# **exit**	Exit class-map configuration mode.

Step 2: Create a Policy

Router(config)# **policy-map LETSQOSEM**	Creates policy LETSQOSEM.

Step 3: Add Class Maps to the Policy and Specify One (or More) Class(es) with Priority Bandwidth

Router(config-pmap)# **class PRECEDENCE5**	Associates class PRECEDENCE5 with policy LETSQOSEM.
Router(config-pmap-c)# **priority percent 10**	Guarantees 10% bandwidth with first priority data handling.
Router(config-pmap-c)# **class PRECEDENCE7**	Associates class PRECEDENCE7 with policy LETSQOSEM.

`Router(config-pmap-c)# bandwidth percent 15`	Sets guaranteed bandwidth to 15 percent.
`Router(config-pmap-c)# class PRECEDENCE3`	Associates class PRECEDENCE3 with policy LETSQOSEM.
`Router(config-pmap-c)# bandwidth percent 30`	Sets guaranteed bandwidth to 30 percent.
`Router(config-pmap-c)# class PRECEDENCE0`	Associates class PRECEDENCE0 with policy LETSQOSEM.
`Router(config-pmap-c)# bandwidth percent 20`	Sets guaranteed bandwidth to 20 percent.
`Router(config-pmap-c)# class class-default`	Associates class class-default with policy LETSQOSEM for unspecified traffic.
`Router(config-pmap-c)# fair-queue 20`	Specifies the number of reserved dynamic queues for unclassified traffic.
`Router(config-pmap-c)# exit`	Returns to config-pmap mode.
`Router(config-pmap)# exit`	Returns to global configuration mode.

Step 4: Apply Queuing Policy to an Interface

`Router(config)# interface FastEthernet 0/0`	Chooses an interface to apply queuing policy.
`Router(config-if)# service-policy output LETSQOSEM`	Applies the queuing policy to outbound traffic.

Step 5: Verify Policy Configuration

`Router# show policy-map interface fastethernet 0/0`	Displays the configurations and statistics of policy maps applied at fastethernet 0/0.

Configuring Low-Latency Queuing (LLQ) with Class-Based Weighted Random Early Detection (CBWRED)

Figure 4-6 is a flowchart showing the architecture of Low-Latency Queuing with Class-Based Weighted Random Early Detection. The configuration that follows the diagram shows a specific example of configuring LLQ with CBWRED.

Figure 4-6 Low-Latency Queuing with Class-Based Weighted Random Early Detection

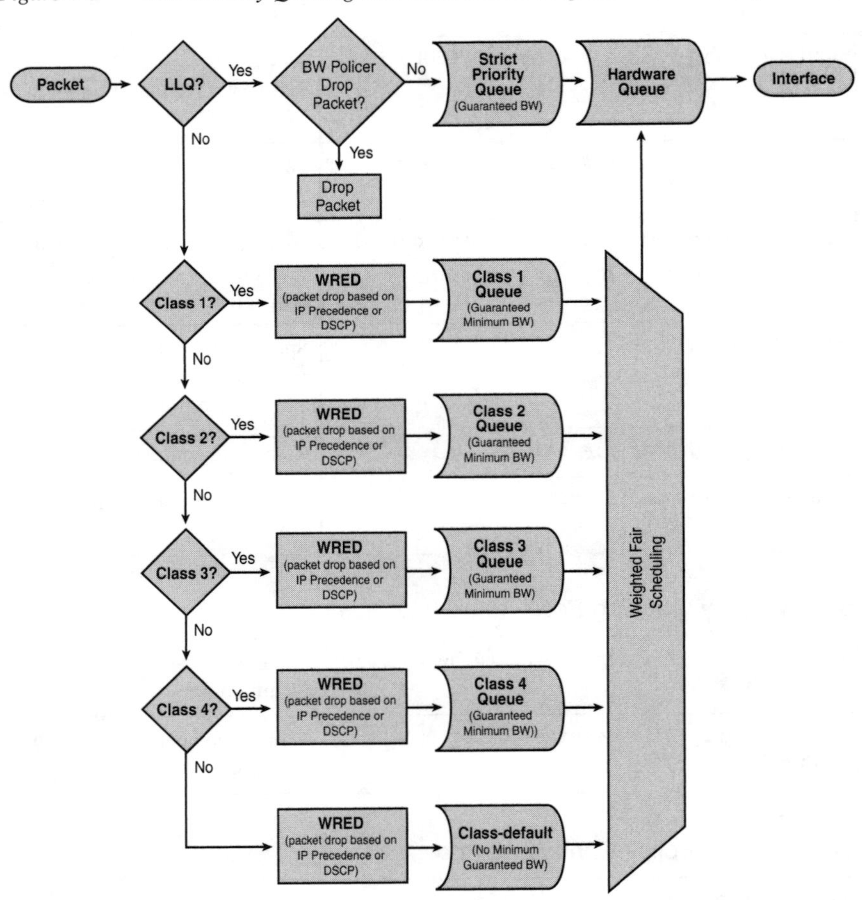

The tasks to configure CBWRED with LLQ are

STEP 1. Define one or more class maps to specify traffic.

STEP 2. Create a policy.

STEP 3. Add class maps to the policy and specify one (or more) class(es) with priority bandwidth.

STEP 4. Apply policy to an interface.

STEP 5. Verify policy configuration.

Step 1: Define One or More Class Maps to Specify Traffic

Router(config-cmap)# **class-map match-any VoIP**	Creates class VoIP.
Router(config-cmap)# **match precedence 5**	Selects traffic with IP precedence 5.
Router(config-cmap)# **class-map match-any CRITICAL**	Creates class CRITICAL.
Router(config-cmap)# **match precedence 3 4**	Selects traffic with IP precedence 3 and 4.
Router(config-cmap)# **class-map match-any NOTCRITICAL**	Creates class NOTCRITICAL.
Router(config-cmap)# **match precedence 1 2**	Selects traffic with IP precedence 1 and 2.
Router(config-cmap)# **exit**	Returns to global configuration mode.

Step 2: Create a Policy

Router(config)# **policy-map POLICY-1**	Creates policy POLICY-1.

Step 3: Add Class Maps to the Policy and Specify One (or More) Class(es) with Priority Bandwidth

Router(config-pmap)# **class VoIP**	Associates class VoIP with policy POLICY-1.
Router(config-pmap-c)# **priority percent 10**	Guarantees 10% bandwidth with first priority data handling.
Router(config-pmap-c)# **class CRITICAL**	Associates class CRITICAL with policy POLICY-1.

Router(config-pmap-c)# **bandwidth percent 15**	Sets guaranteed bandwidth to 15 percent.
Router(config-pmap-c)# **random-detect**	Enables Random Early Detection.
Router(config-pmap-c)# **random-detect precedence 3 26 40 10**	Sets minimum (26 packets) and maximum (40 packets) drop thresholds for traffic with default mark-prob-denominator of 10 for precedence value 3.
Router(config-pmap-c)# **random-detect precedence 4 28 40 10**	Sets minimum (28 packets) and maximum (40 packets) drop thresholds for traffic with default mark-prob-denominator of 10 for precedence value 4.
	NOTE: The DSCP-based random detect can apply a minimum drop threshold level, maximum drop threshold level, and mark-probability-denominator for each or any DSCP value within a queue or class.
Router(config-pmap-c)# **class NOTCRITICAL**	Associates class NOTCRITICAL with policy POLICY-1.
Router(config-pmap-c)# **bandwidth percent 30**	Sets guaranteed bandwidth to 30 percent.
Router(config-pmap-c)# **random-detect**	Enables Random Early Detection.
Router(config-pmap-c)# **random-detect precedence 1 22 36 10**	Sets minimum (22 packets) and maximum (36 packets) drop thresholds for traffic with default mark-prob-denominator of 10 for precedence value 1.
Router(config-pmap-c)# **random-detect precedence 2 24 36 10**	Sets minimum (24 packets) and maximum (36 packets) drop thresholds for traffic with default mark-prob-denominator of 10 for precedence value 2.

Router(config-pmap-c)# **class class-default**	Associates class class-default with policy POLICY-1 for unspecified traffic.
Router(config-pmap-c)# **fair-queue 20**	Specifies the number of reserved dynamic queues for unclassified traffic.
Router(config-pmap-c)# **random-detect**	Enables WRED with defaults for the "catch remaining traffic" default class.
Router(config-pmap-c)# **exit**	Returns to Config-pmap mode.
Router(config-pmap)# **exit**	Returns to global configuration mode.

Step 4: Apply Policy to an Interface

Router(config)# **interface fastethernet 0/0**	Chooses an interface to apply queuing policy.
Router(config-if)# **service-policy output POLICY-1**	Applies the queuing policy to outbound traffic.

Step 5: Verify Policy Configuration

Router# **show policy-map interface fastethernet 0/0**	Displays the configurations and statistics of policy maps applied at fastethernet 0/0.

NOTE: WRED is IP precedence-based by default, but it can be configured to be DSCP-based, if desired.

WRED has three configuration parameters: minimum threshold, maximum threshold, and mark probability denominator (MPD). If the size of the queue is smaller than the minimum threshold, packets are not dropped. As the size of the queue grows beyond the minimum threshold, the rate of packet drops also increases. If the size of the queue becomes larger than the maximum threshold, all arriving packets are dropped. The minimum and maximum threshold ranges are 1 to 4096.

MPD is an integer that dictates to drop 1 of the MPD when the size of the queue is between the minimum and maximum thresholds. For example, if the MPD is set to 10, and the queue size is between minimum and maximum values, there is a drop of 1 out of every 10 packets. The value of the mark probability can range from 1 to 65,535.

With WRED you can set up a different profile (with a minimum threshold, maximum threshold, and MPD) for each traffic priority.

Traffic Policing

Traffic policing drops excess traffic to control traffic flow within specified rate limits. Traffic policing does not introduce any delay to traffic that conforms to traffic policies. Traffic policing can cause more TCP retransmissions, because traffic in excess of specified limits is dropped.

Single Token Bucket/Single Rate

NOTE: Traffic policing is configured in a traffic policy in the policy-map class configuration mode.

The command syntax for the **police** command is:

```
Router(config-pmap-c)# police bps [burst-normal] [burst-max]
conform-action action exceed-action action [violate-action action]
```

The following explains the syntax:

bps	Average rate in bits per second. Valid values are 8000 to 200000000.
burst-normal	Normal burst size in bytes. Valid values are 1000 to 51200000. The default normal burst size is 1500 bytes.
burst-max	Excess burst size in bytes. Valid values are 1000 to 51200000.
conform-action *action*	Action to take on packets that conform to the rate limit.
exceed-action *action*	Action to take on packets that exceed the rate limit.
violate-action *action*	Action to take on packets that violate the normal and maximum burst sizes.

NOTE: The command syntax of the **police** command allows you to specify the action to be taken on a packet when you enable the *action* keyword. The resulting action corresponding to the keyword choices are as follows:

action **Keyword**	**Resulting Action**
`drop`	Drops the packet.
`set-prec-transmit` *new-prec*	Sets the IP precedence and sends the packet.
`set-qos-transmit` *new-qos*	Sets the QoS group and sends the packet.
`set-dscp-transmit` *new-dscp*	Sets the differentiated services code point (DSCP) value and sends the packet.
`transmit`	Sends the packet.

NOTE: A single-token bucket system is used when the **violate-action** option is not specified, and a two-token bucket system is used when the **violate-action** option is specified.

Router(config)# **class-map BWHUNGRY-1**	Creates class map BWHUNGRY-1.
Router(config-cmap)# **match access-group 99**	Chooses traffic using access list 99.
Router(config-cmap)# **exit**	Exits class map mode.
Router(config)# **policy-map NOUDONT-1**	Creates a policy named NOUDONT-1.
Router(config-pmap)# **class BWHUNGRY-1**	Chooses a class to apply policy.
Router(config-pmap-c)# **police 10000 5000 10000 conform-action transmit exceed-action set-qos-transmit 4**	Sets the average data rate at 10 kbps for forwarding with a normal burst of 5 kbps and maximum burst of 10 kbps. The conform action is transmit and the non-conforming action sets the qos group value to 4 and then transmits.
Router(config-pmap-c)# **exit**	Returns to config-pmap mode.
Router(config-pmap)# **exit**	Returns to global configuration mode.

Router(config)# **interface fastethernet 0/0**	Enters interface mode where the policy will be applied.
Router(config-if)# **service-policy input** NOUDONT-1	Applies policy NOUDONT-1.
Router(config-if)# **end**	Returns to privileged mode.
Router# **show policy-map**	Displays all configured policy maps on the device.
Router# **show policy-map** NOUDONT-1	Displays the policy map NOUDONT-1.
Router# **show policy-map interface fastethernet 0/0**	Displays the configurations and statistics of policy maps applied at fastethernet 0/0.

Two Token Bucket/Two Rate

The two rate policer polices both committed information rate (CIR) and peak information rate (PIR) using two token buckets. In this case, the command syntax is

```
Router(config-pmap-c)# police cir cir [bc conform-burst] pir pir [be
peak-burst]
[conform-action action [exceed-action action [violate-action
action]]]
```

The following explains the syntax:

cir *cir*	CIR value in bits per second (8000 to 200,000,000).
bc *conform-burst*	Conform burst (bc) size used by the first token bucket for policing.
pir *pir*	Peak information rate (PIR) at which the second token bucket is updated.
be *peak-burst*	Peak burst (be) size in bytes.
conform-action *action*	Action to take on packets that conform to the CIR and PIR.
exceed-action *action*	Action to take on packets that conform to the PIR but not the CIR.
violate-action *action*	Action to take on packets that exceed the PIR.

NOTE: Traffic policing is configured in a traffic policy in the policy-map class configuration mode.

A single-token bucket system is used when the **violate-action** option is not specified, and a two-token bucket system is used when the **violate-action** option is specified.

`Router(config)#` **`class-map BWHUNGRY-2`**	Creates class map BWHUNGRY-2.
`Router(config-cmap)#` **`match access-group 101`**	Chooses traffic using access list 101.
`Router(config-cmap)#` **`exit`**	Exits class map mode.
`Router(config)#` **`policy-map NOUDONT-2`**	Creates a policy named NOUDONT-2.
`Router(config-pmap)#` **`class BWHUNGRY-2`**	Chooses a class to apply policy.
`Router(config-pmap-c)#` **`police cir 200000 bc 10000 pir 700000 be 10000 conform-action transmit exceed-action set-prec-transmit 2 violate-action drop`**	Sets **cir** data rate at 200 kbps for forwarding with policing. There is a burst overage of 10 kbps. A **pir** data rate is set to 700 kbps and peak burst of 10 kbps. Nonconformance of either **cir** or **pir** resets precedence value to 2 and violation of either **bc** or **be** forces a packet drop.
`Router(config-pmap-c)#` **`exit`**	Returns to config-pmap mode.
`Router(config-pmap)#` **`exit`**	Returns to global configuration mode.
`Router(config)#` **`interface fastethernet 0/0`**	Enters interface mode where the policy will be applied.
`Router(config-if)#` **`service-policy input NOUDONT-2`**	Applies policy NOUDONT-2.
`Router(config-if)#` **`end`**	Returns to privileged mode.
`Router#` **`show policy-map`**	Displays all configured policy maps on the device.
`Router#` **`show policy-map NOUDONT-2`**	Displays the policy map NOUDONT-2.
`Router#` **`show policy-map interface fastethernet 0/0`**	Displays the configurations and statistics of policy maps applied at fastethernet 0/0.

Traffic Shaping

Traffic shaping is typically used to prevent and manage congestion in ATM, Frame Relay, or Metro Ethernet networks, where asymmetric bandwidths are used along the traffic path. Traffic shaping is performed on outbound traffic of an interface.

Per-Interface Traffic Shaping

The command syntax for the **traffic-shape rate** command is

Router(config-if)# **traffic-shape rate** *bit-rate* [*burst-size* [*excess-burst-size*]][*buffer-limit*]

bit-rate	Bit rate that traffic is shaped to, in bits per second.
burst-size	Sustained number of bits that can be sent per interval.
excess-burst-size	Maximum number of bits that can exceed the burst size in the first interval in a congestion event.
buffer-limit	Maximum buffer limit in bps. Valid entries are numbers in the range of 0 to 4096.

NOTE: Both *burst-size* and *excess-burst-size* are *not* measured in bits per second but rather the number of bits counted in a prescribed timing interval.

Router>**enable**	Enables privileged EXEC mode.
Router# **configure terminal**	Enters global configuration mode.
Router(config)# **interface serial 0/0/0**	Enters interface configuration mode.
Router(config-if)# **traffic-shape rate 250000 4000 8000**	Enables traffic shaping for outbound traffic based on the bit rate specified.
Router(config-if)# **end**	Returns to privileged EXEC mode.

Class-Based Traffic Shaping

NOTE: Class-based traffic shaping applies to outbound traffic only.

The command syntax for the **shape** command is

`Router(config-pmap-c)# shape {average | peak} cir [bc] [be]`

The following explains the syntax:

average	Specifies average rate shaping.
peak	Specifies peak rate shaping.
cir	The committed information rate (CIR), in bits per second (bps).
bc	The committed burst size, in bits.
be	The excess burst size, in bits.

Router(config)# **class-map 2BWHUNGRY**	Creates class map 2BWHUNGRY.
Router(config-cmap)# **match protocol pop3**	Chooses traffic by protocol.
Router(config-cmap)# **exit**	Exits class map mode.
Router(config)# **policy-map NOTU2**	Creates a policy named NOTU2.
Router(config-pmap)# **class 2BWHUNGRY**	Chooses a class to apply policy.
Router(config-pmap-c)# **shape average 128000 6000 3000**	Shapes traffic at an average of 128 kbps with a committed burst size of 6000 bits and an excess burst size of 3000 bits.
Router(config-pmap-c)# **exit**	Returns to config-pmap mode.
Router(config-pmap)# **exit**	Returns to global configuration mode.

Router(config)# **interface serial 0/0**	Enters interface mode where the policy will be applied.
Router(config-if)# **service-policy out NOTU2**	Applies policy NOTU2.
Router(config-if)# **end**	Returns to privileged mode.
Router# **show policy-map**	Displays all configured policy maps on the device.
Router# **show policy-map NOTU2**	Displays the policy map NOTU2.
Router# **show policy-map interface fastethernet 0/0**	Displays the configurations and statistics of policy maps applied at fastethernet 0/0.

Implementing QoS Preclassify

Quality of service (QoS) preclassify is designed for tunnel interfaces. When the feature is enabled, the QoS features on the output interface classify packets before encryption, allowing traffic flows to be managed in congested environments. The result is more effective packet tunneling.

NOTE: The **qos pre-classify** command is restricted to IP packets defined in crypto maps, tunnel interfaces, and virtual templates.

Router(config)# **interface serial 2/0**	Enters interface configuration mode.
Router(config-if)# **ip address 10.1.1.1**	Assigns a physical interface IP address.
Router(config-if)# **service-policy output 2HEADQ**	Applies a service policy to the interface.
	NOTE: The policy "2HEADQ" (not shown) implements a QoS strategy for marked traffic destined for a GRE/IPSec tunnel.
Router(config-if)# **exit**	Returns to global configuration mode.
Router(config)# **interface tunnel1**	Creates a GRE tunnel.

Router(config-if)# **ip address 172.16.1.1**	Assigns the tunnel IP address.
Router(config-if)# **tunnel source serial 2/0**	Assigns the tunnel source interface.
Router(config-if)# **tunnel destination 172.16.1.2**	Configures the tunnel's IP endpoint.
Router(config-if)# **crypto map CLOWNS**	Applies a crypto map to the GRE tunnel interface.
Router(config-if)# **qos pre-classify**	Classifies packet on its pre-tunnel attributes.
Router(config-if)# **exit**	Returns to global configuration mode.
Router(config)# **crypto map CLOWNS 10 ipsec-isakmp**	Creates crypto map CLOWNS.
Router(config-crypto-map)# **set peer 10.1.1.2**	Configures the destination peer of the IPSec tunnel.
Router(config-crypto-map)# **set transform-set HEADQ**	Declares a transform set.
Router(config-crypto-map)# **match ip address 101**	Chooses the tunnel traffic using access-list 101.
Router(config-crypto-map)# **qos pre-classify**	Classifies packet on its pre-tunnel attributes.
Router(config-crypto-map)# **exit**	Returns to global configuration mode.

CHAPTER 5

AutoQoS

This chapter provides information and commands concerning the following topics:

- Forms of AutoQoS
- Locations Where AutoQoS Can Be Implemented
- Serial Interface Restrictions
- Frame Relay DLCI and ATM Restrictions
- Router Design Considerations
- Router Prerequisites
- Deploying AutoQoS on Routers
- Deploying AutoQoS on IOS-Based Catalyst Switches
- Verifying Cisco AutoQoS on the Router
- Verifying Cisco AutoQoS on the Switch
- Flowchart for Verifying and Modifying AutoQoS-Generated Configurations

Forms of AutoQoS

The two forms of AutoQoS are

- **AutoQoS VoIP**:
  - — Developed to automate IP telephony deployments for those with limited experience
  - — One deployment stage
  - — Works on both routers and switches
  - — Uses NBAR for classification and marking of packet DiffServ Codepoint (DSCP) fields
  - — Can trust packet markings and not re-mark them
- **AutoQoS Enterprise**:
  - — Available only on routers
  - — Added capabilities above AutoQoS VoIP for voice, video, data, and protocol discovery
  - — Two deployment stages: 1. Discovering types and volumes of traffic and generating policies; 2. Implementing the generated policies

Locations Where AutoQoS Can Be Implemented

AutoQoS Enterprise can be implemented on the following types of router interfaces and PVCs only:

- Serial interfaces with PPP or HDLC encapsulation
- Frame Relay point-to-point subinterfaces (multipoint is not supported)
- ATM point-to-point subinterfaces (PVCs) on both slow (768 kbps or lower) and fast (above 768 kbps) serial interfaces
- Frame Relay-to-ATM internetworking links

Serial Interface Restrictions

Restrictions of AutoQoS on serial links are

- On low-speed (768 kbps or lower) serial links, AutoQoS must be enabled on both ends.
  — Configured bandwidths must be consistent.
- Multilink PPP (MLP) is enabled automatically.
  — When MLP is configured, the IP address of the interface is removed and put onto the virtual template (MLP bundle).

Frame Relay DLCI and ATM Restrictions

Restrictions of AutoQoS on Frame Relay DLCIs and ATM PVCs are

- AutoQoS cannot be implemented on a DLCI if a map class is attached to the DLCI.
- AutoQoS cannot be implemented on a low-speed DLCI (768 kbps or lower) if a virtual template is already configured for the DLCI.
- If a Frame Relay DLCI is already assigned to one subinterface, you cannot configure AutoQoS VoIP from a different subinterface.
- For a low-speed DLCI (768 kbps or lower) configured with FR-to-ATM internetworking, MLP is configured automatically; the subinterface must have an IP address.
- When MLP over FR is configured, the IP address is removed and placed on the MLP bundle.
- AutoQoS cannot be implemented on a low-speed ATM PVC if a virtual template is already configured for the ATM PVC.
- For a low-speed ATM PVC, MLP over ATM is configured automatically; the subinterface must have an IP address.
- When MLP over ATM is configured, the IP address is removed and placed on the MLP bundle.

Router Design Considerations

Depending on the interface type, bandwidth, and encapsulation, AutoQoS may enable different features on the router interfaces:

- **Low-Latency Queuing (LLC):**
  - — Reserves a priority queue for VoIP (RTP) traffic, providing a guaranteed but policed bandwidth.
  - — Other queues serve other traffic with specific bandwidth guarantees, but defer to the priority queue.
- **Compressed RTP (cRTP):**
  - — Reduces the IP/UDP/RTP header from 40 bytes down to 2 bytes (without CRC) or 4 bytes (with CRC)
  - — Used on low-speed serial interfaces
  - — Improves link efficiency
  - — Must be applied at both ends of the link
- **Link Fragmentation and Interleaving (LFI):**
  - — Fragments large data packets on slow interfaces
  - — Reduces jitter; voice packets will not be delayed by large data packets in the queue
  - — Must be applied on both ends of the link

Router Prerequisites

Before configuring AutoQoS on a router, the following prerequisites must be met:

- Cisco Express Forwarding (CEF) must be enabled on the interface where AutoQoS is to be enabled.
  - — AutoQoS relies on NBAR for discovery, and NBAR needs CEF.
- You cannot apply a QoS policy (service policy) to the interface prior to enabling AutoQoS on that interface.
- You must configure the bandwidth on all interfaces and subinterfaces.
  - — On slow links (768 kbps or lower), you must configure an IP address.
  - — AutoQoS enables MLP on slow links and moves the IP address to the MLP virtual template.
- For AutoQoS SNMP traps to work, you must have SNMP enabled on the router and specify the server address for SNMP traps destination.
  - — The address must be reachable from the router.
  - — The SNMP community string "AutoQoS" must have write permission.

- By default, Cisco routers reserve up to 75 percent of the interface bandwidth for user-defined classes.
  - — The remaining bandwidth is kept for the default class.
  - — The entire remaining bandwidth is not guaranteed to the default class.
  - — The default class and excess traffic from other bandwidth classes share this bandwidth proportionately.

Deploying AutoQoS on Routers

Deploying AutoQoS for the Enterprise on Cisco routers is a two-step process:

STEP 1. Auto Discovery

STEP 2. Generation and deployment of either AutoQoS Enterprise or AutoQoS VoIP

Step 1: Auto Discovery

`Router(config)#`**`interface fastethernet 0/0`**	Moves to interface configuration mode.
`Router(config-if)#`**`auto discovery qos`**	Begins the Auto-Discovery process of AutoQoS, using NBAR, to collect data and analyze interface egress traffic for packet classification.
`Router(config-if)#`**`auto discovery qos trust`**	Begins the Auto-Discovery process of AutoQoS. The **trust** keyword indicates the existing DSCP markings should not be altered. NBAR is not used.
`Router(config-if)#`**`no auto discovery`** `[`**`trust`**`]`	Stops auto discovery (data collection) and removes any reports that have been generated.
`Router#`**`show auto discovery qos`**	Shows the results of the auto discovery while discovery is in progress.

NOTE: The longer the auto discovery runs, the more accurate the results will be. The default period is three (3) days.

NOTE: The **auto discovery qos** command is not supported on subinterfaces. The **auto discovery qos** command is also not supported on an interface that has a policy attached to it already.

Step 2: Generation and Deployment of AutoQoS Enterprise

`Router(config)#interface serial 0/0`	Moves to interface configuration mode.
`Router(config-if)#auto qos`	Enables AutoQoS to create class maps and policy maps for the enterprise feature at the interface upon completion of Step 1: Auto Discovery.

Step 2: Generation and Deployment of AutoQoS VoIP

`Router(config)#interface serial 0/0`	Moves to interface configuration mode.
`Router(config-if)#auto qos [voip [trust] [fr-atm]]`	Enables AutoQoS with the VoIP feature at the interface upon completion of Step 1: Auto Discovery.
	NOTE: Use the keyword **voip** if you are enabling AutoQoS VoIP instead of AutoQoS Enterprise. AutoQoS VoIP does not require the discovery step.
	NOTE: Use the keyword **trust** if you want to use the preset markings of the packets rather than ignoring them and classifying them with NBAR.
	NOTE: Use the keyword **fr-atm** if you are enabling AutoQoS VoIP for Frame Relay-to-ATM internetworking.

Deploying AutoQoS on IOS-Based Catalyst Switches

NOTE: Catalyst LAN Switches will support only AutoQoS VoIP.

NOTE: Catalyst LAN Switches with the Catalyst operating system are configured differently than IOS-based switches. The ONT exam focuses on IOS-based switches—2960(EI), 3560, and 4500 in particular, although the 6500 is sometimes referenced. Note that the 2950/2960 switches require the Enhanced Image (EI) and not the Standard Image (SI) for AutoQoS VoIP.

NOTE: AutoQoS VoIP support for IP softphone is only available on the 6500 series switch, and not on the 2960/3560/4500 series.

Enabling AutoQoS VoIP on Cisco switches involves two different commands:

- Command 1: Enabling AutoQoS on access ports to which either a workstation or an IP phone is connected
- Command 2: Enabling AutoQoS on ports that are connected to other trusted devices such as routers and switches

NOTE: A trusted device is one whose marked traffic is honored by the local device.

Command 1: Enabling AutoQoS on Access Ports to Which Either a Workstation or an IP Phone Is Connected

`Switch(config-if)#`**`auto qos voip cisco-phone`**	Configures the QoS on the port and enables the trusted boundary feature for a Cisco VoIP phone.

NOTE: The trusted boundary feature uses CDP to detect the presence or absence of a Cisco IP phone. When AutoQoS detects a Cisco IP phone, the ingress classification on the interface is set to trust the QoS label received in the packet. When a Cisco IP phone is absent, AutoQoS sets the ingress classification to not trust the QoS label in the packet. It also reconfigures the egress queues on the interface. This command extends the trust boundary if an IP phone is detected.

NOTE: Cisco Discovery Protocol version 2 (CDPv2) must be enabled on the interface. CDPv2 is used to determine whether a Cisco IP phone is connected to the port.

Command 2: Enabling AutoQoS on Ports That Are Connected to Other Trusted Devices Such as Routers and Switches

`Switch(config-if)#`**`auto qos voip trust`**	Configures QoS on the port and extends the QoS trust boundary to a connected device.

NOTE: This interface is usually an uplink trunk connection to another switch or router. The **auto qos voip trust** command also reconfigures the egress queues on the interfaces where it was applied.

Verifying Cisco AutoQoS on the Router

Router#**show auto qos**	Displays the AutoQoS templates and initial router configuration.
Router#**show auto qos interface serial 0/0/0**	Displays the AutoQoS templates and initial router configuration for the specified router interface.
Router#**show auto discovery qos**	Displays the results as found by the autodiscovery.
Router#**show auto discovery qos interface serial 0/0/0**	Displays the results as found by the autodiscovery for the specified router interface.
Router#**show policy-map interface serial 0/0/0**	Displays the autogenerated policies and QoS parameters for the specified router interface.

Verifying Cisco AutoQoS on the Switch

Switch#**show auto qos**	Displays the AutoQoS templates and initial switch configuration.
Switch#**show auto qos interface serial 0/0/0**	Displays the AutoQoS templates and initial switch configuration for the specified interface.
Switch#**show mls qos maps cos-dscp**	Displays the switch's layer 2 CoS to the layer 3 DSCP mapping table.
Switch#**show mls qos maps dscp-cos**	Displays the switch's layer 3 DSCP to the layer 2 CoS mapping table.
Switch#**show mls qos interface fastethernet 0/1**	Displays QoS information for the specified switch interface.
Switch#**show mls qos vlan 10**	Displays the QoS policy map information for the specified SVI, VLAN 10.

Flowchart for Verifying and Modifying AutoQoS-Generated Configurations

AutoQoS was developed to help automate QoS configuration for common scenarios. The configuration that AutoQoS generates may not be suitable for your network. The flowchart in Figure 5-1 shows some possible paths that you might follow in using AutoQoS and verifying its auto-generated commands, as well as steps to modifying the command, if necessary.

Figure 5-1 Verify and Modify AutoQoS-Generated Configuration

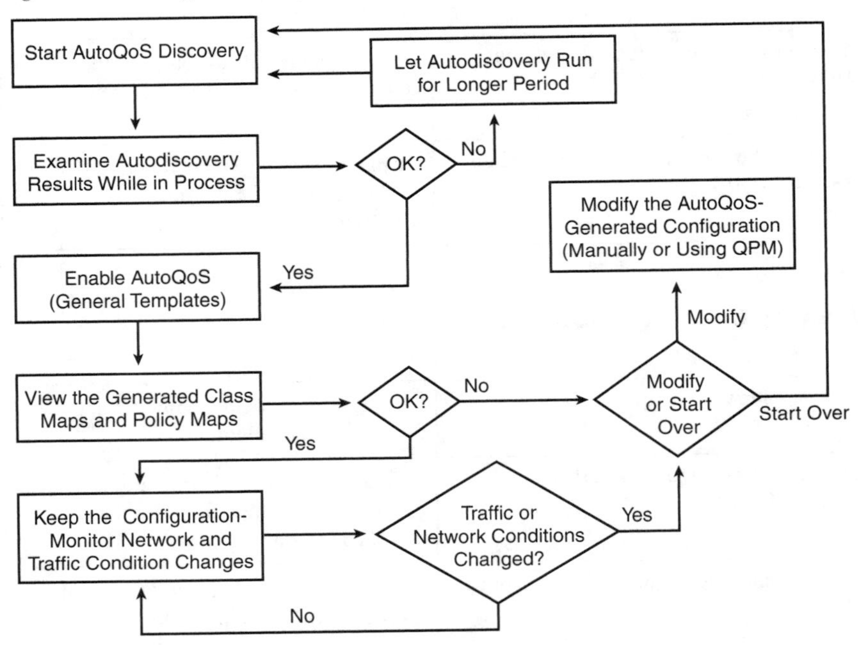

The procedure can be summarized into three steps:

STEP 1. Review the existing QoS policy, identify new requirements, and outline the modifications necessary.

STEP 2. Modify the AutoQoS-generated configuration according to new requirements identified in Step 1.

STEP 3. Review the new (modified) configuration.

TIP: If you modify the AutoQoS-generated configuration, and you later decide to remove the configuration with the **no auto qos** command, the modifications will not be removed. Only the original, unmodified commands that AutoQoS generated will be removed.

CHAPTER 6

Wireless Scalability

This chapter provides information and commands concerning the following topics:

- Wireless LAN QoS Configuration Using the GUI
- Configuring Encryption and Authentication on Lightweight Access Points
  - — Configuring Open Authentication
  - — Configuring Static WEP Authentication
  - — Configuring WPA with PSK
  - — Configuring Web Authentication
  - — Configuring 802.1x Authentication
- Cisco Wireless Control System (WCS)
  - — WCS Login
  - — WCS Summary Pages
  - — Changing the Root Password
  - — Adding a Cisco Wireless LAN Controller
  - — Configuring Access Points
  - — WCS Maps—Adding a Campus Map
  - — WCS Maps—Adding a New Building
  - — Rogue Access Point Detection

Wireless LAN QoS Configuration Using the GUI

All Cisco WLAN controllers (WLC) have a built-in GUI that can be used to configure and manage the device. Figure 6-1 shows the GUI for a Cisco 4402 (WLC) after a successful login.

Figure 6-1 4402 WLC GUI After Login

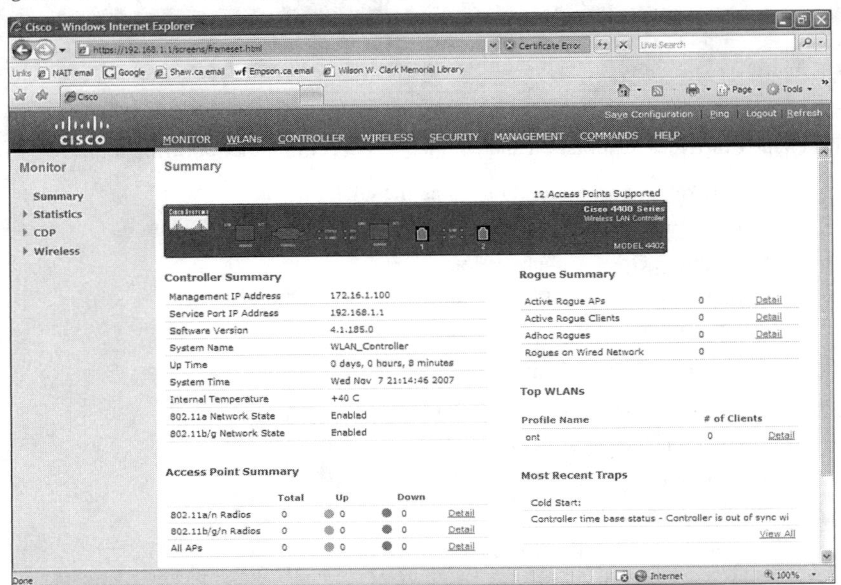

On the menu bar on the top of the screen, click **Controller**. The Controller option has many pages that you can go to, including the QoS section. On the left side of the page, on the vertical menu, click **QoS**. This expands to show the QoS menu, which has one item: **Profiles**. Clicking **Profiles** opens the QoS Profiles page, as shown in Figure 6-2.

Clicking any of the profiles on this page takes you to a new web page that allows you to edit the specified profile. Figure 6-3 shows the Edit QoS Profile page for the Bronze profile.

Figure 6-2 QoS Profiles Page

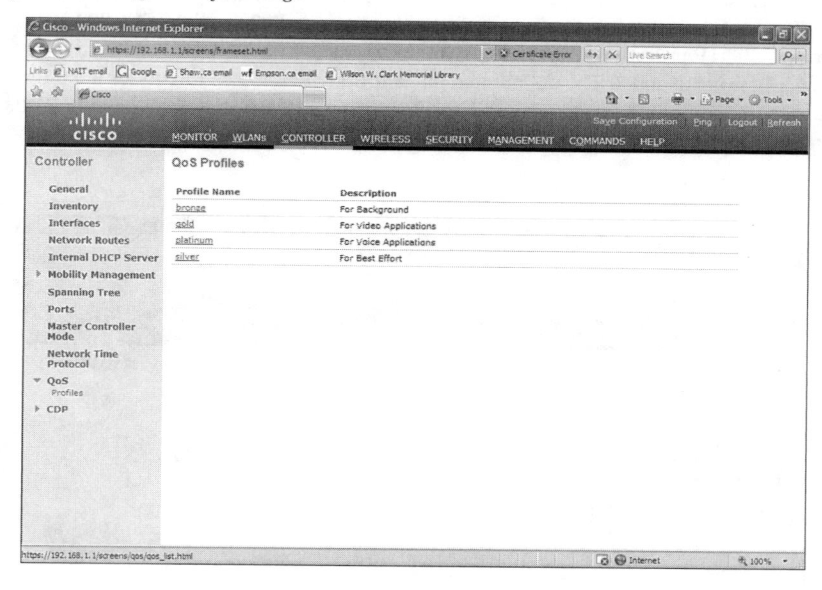

Figure 6-3 Edit QoS Profile Page

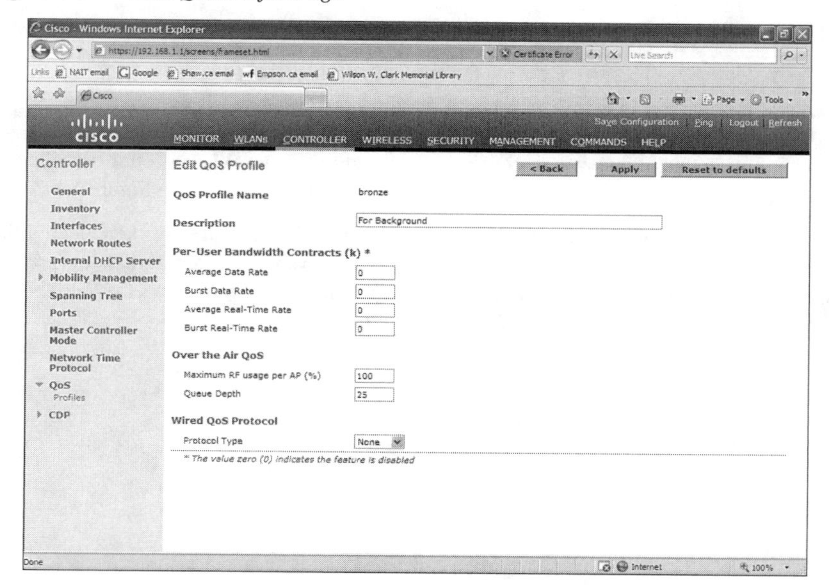

On the Edit QoS Profile page, on the bottom of the main section is a section named Wired QoS Protocol. In this section you can select either **none** or **802.1p**. Selecting **802.1p** activates 802.1P priority tags and allows you to set the tag for the wired connection to a number between **0** and **7**. The default mappings for the four access categories are **6** for Platinum, **5** for Gold, **3** for Silver, and **1** for Bronze. Figure 6-4 shows this section of the Edit QoS Profiles page.

Figure 6-4 Wired QoS Protocol 802.1P Settings

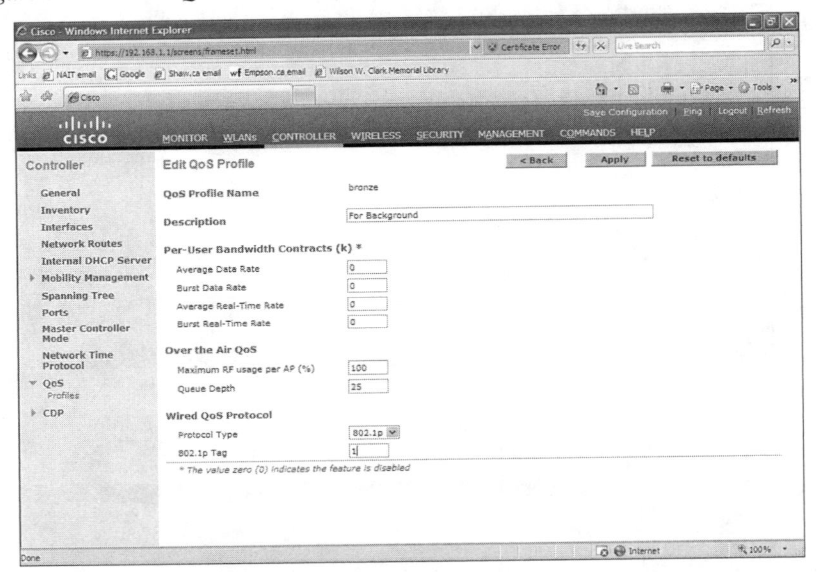

Another option that allows you to configure QoS settings is the **WLANs** option on the top of the page. Selecting **WLANs** opens a page similar to the one shown in Figure 6-5.

The WLAN page shows all the WLAN profiles that have been created so far. Clicking the **New** button in the upper-right hand side of the page allows you to configure a new profile. Clicking the profile name allows you to edit this profile. Figure 6-6 shows the WLANs > Edit page for the profile named ‘ont’ from Figure 6-5.

Figure 6-5 WLAN Settings

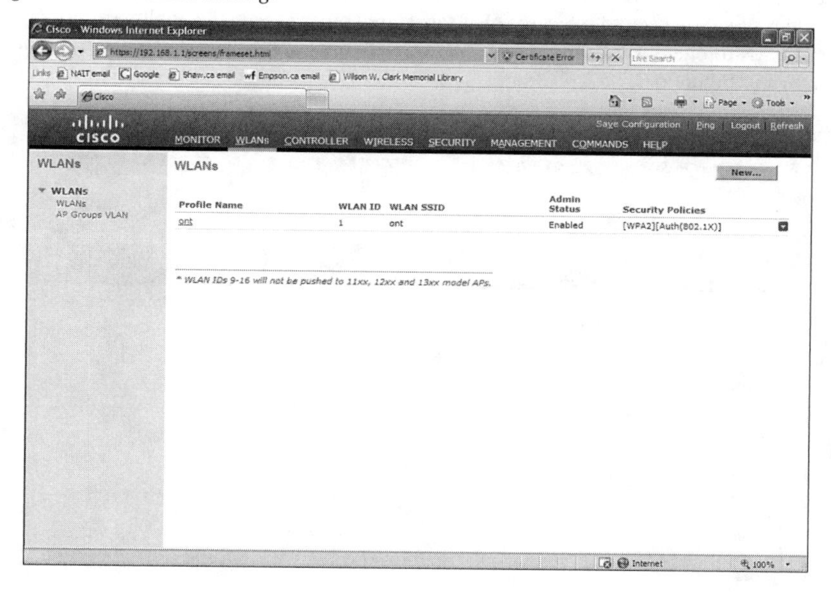

Figure 6-6 WLANs > Edit Page

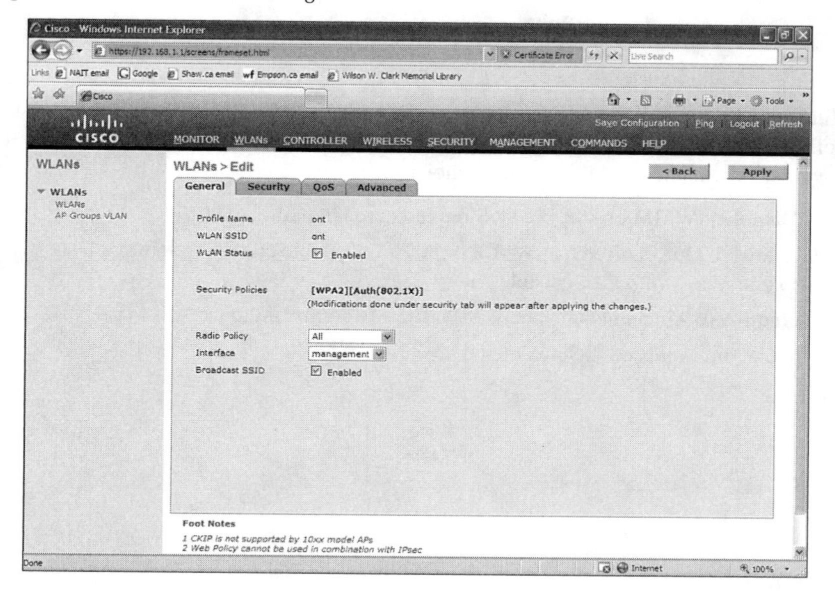

The WLANs > Edit page has four tabs from which to choose when editing your configuration. You want to select the **QoS** tab. Here you can select the quality of service for this WLAN to one of **Platinum**, **Gold**, **Silver**, or **Bronze**. This drop-down menu for QoS is shown in Figure 6-7.

Figure 6-7 WLAN QoS

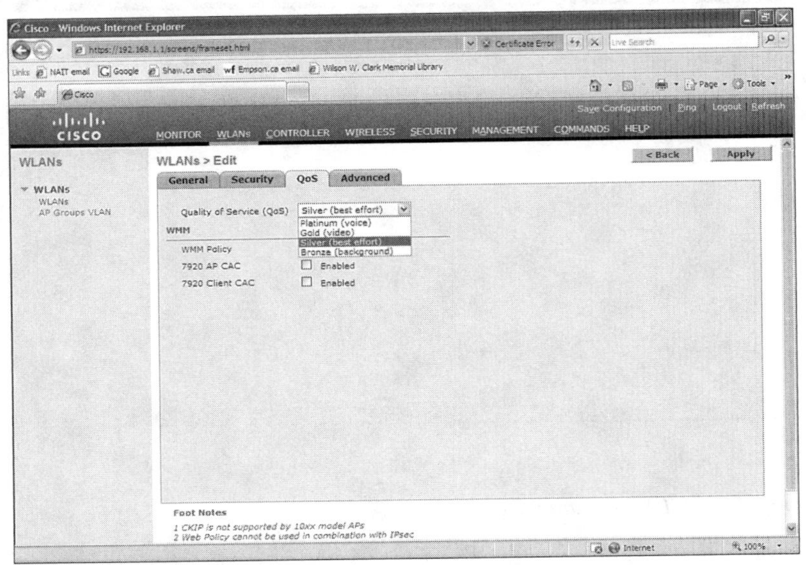

Hidden under the drop-down menu in Figure 6-7 was the drop-down menu for the WMM policy. Here you have three choices for the WMM or 802.11e policy for interaction between a wireless client and the AP. Your three choices are

- **Disabled**: WMM or 802.11e QoS requests are ignored.
- **Allowed**: QoS is offered to WMM or 802.11e-capable clients. Default QoS is offered to non-WMM/802.11e-capable clients.
- **Required**: All clients must be WMM/802.11e compliant to use this WLAN ID.

Figure 6-8 shows this drop-down menu.

Figure 6-8 WMM Policy

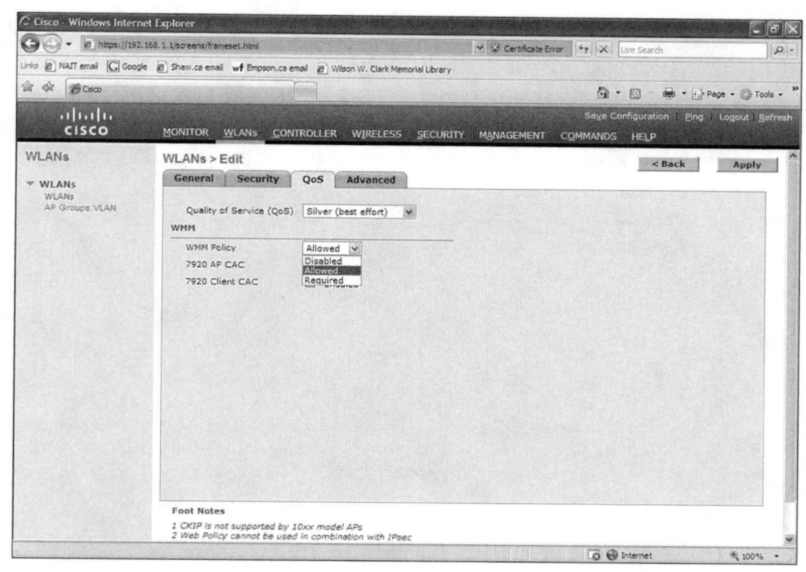

Configuring Encryption and Authentication on Lightweight Access Points

> **NOTE:** Using the GUI of a Wireless LAN Controller (WLC) to configure encryption and authentication on a Lightweight AP is possible. The screenshots in these sections are taken from a Cisco 4402 WLC.

From the main page of the WLC GUI, click **WLANs** on the top menu bar to go to the WLAN section. If you need to create a new WLAN, click **New** on the upper-right hand side, enter in the WLAN ID number, profile name, and SSID, and then click **Apply** to move to the WLAN Edit page. Figure 6-9 shows the screen to create a new WLAN, while Figure 6-10 shows the WLANs > Edit screen.

Figure 6-9 Create a New WLAN Profile

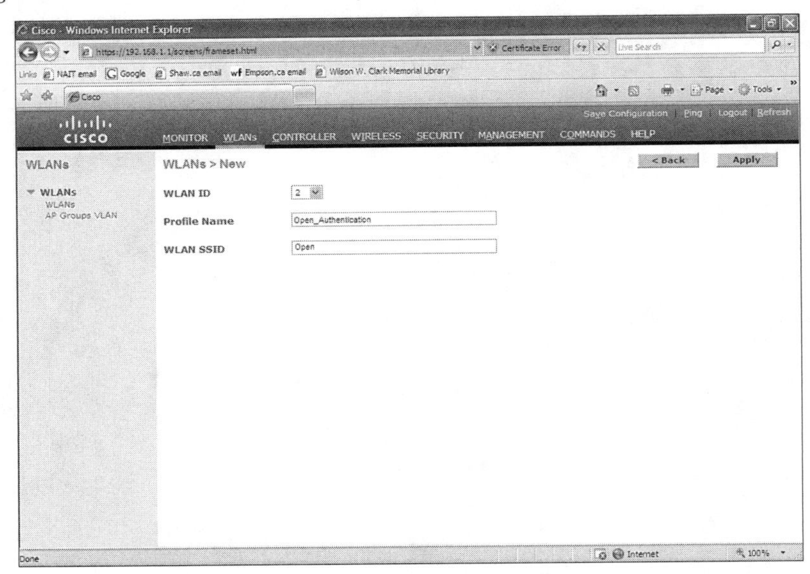

Figure 6-10 Edit a WLAN

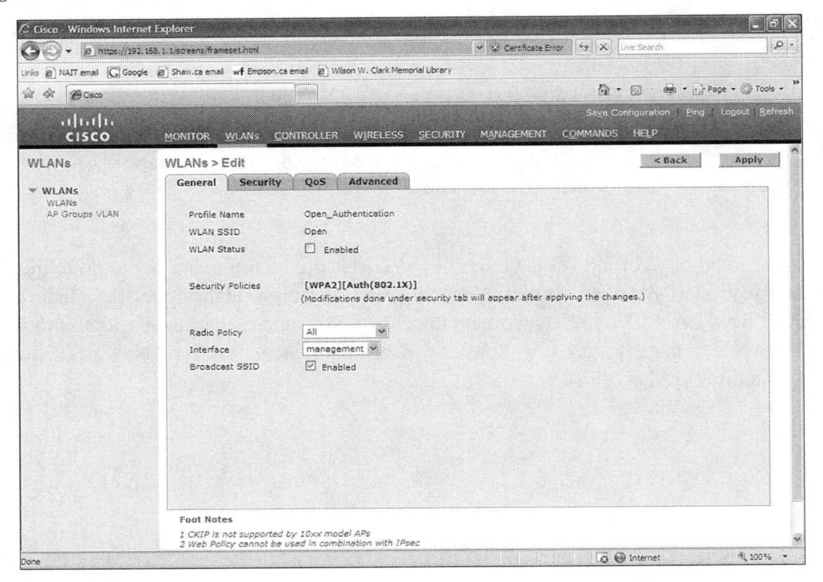

Configuring Open Authentication

Open authentication is used when no authentication or encryption is desired. It is often used in public places or hotspots.

For existing WLANs, click the name of the WLAN you want to edit. If you need to create a new WLAN, follow the steps as shown in the previous section, using Figures 6-9 and 6-10 as a reference.

To edit the security settings of the WLAN, click the **Security** tab as shown in Figure 6-11. You need to go to the drop-down menu for Layer 2 security, and choose **None**. Depending on the security policy options selected, the bottom of the page will change. Click the **Layer 3** tab to ensure that the security field here is also set to **None**, as shown in Figure 6-12. Click **Apply** when you are finished to return to the main WLAN page.

Figure 6-11 Layer 2 Security

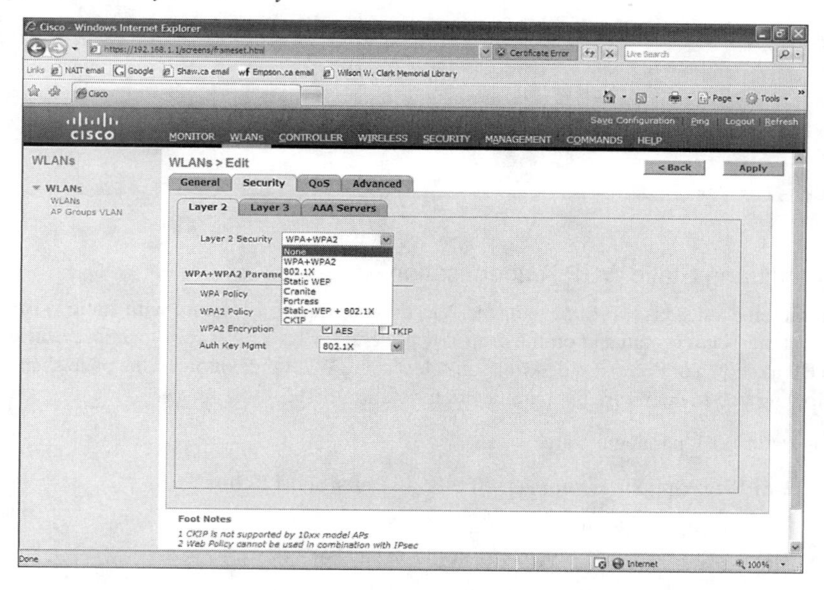

Figure 6-12 Layer 3 Security

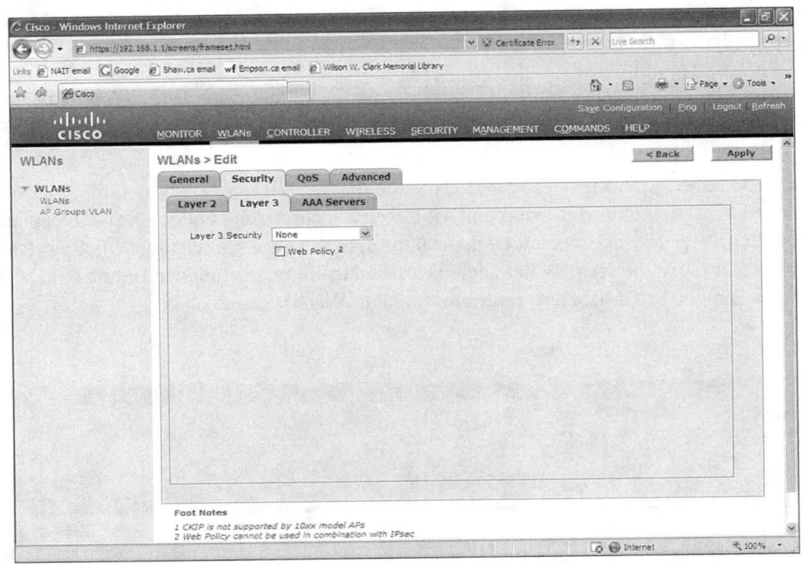

Configuring Static WEP Authentication

Start on the WLANs > Edit page of the WLAN you want to configure with static WEP. Select the **Security** tab and on the drop-down menu for Layer 2 security, choose **Static WEP** as shown in Figure 6-13. After you select static WEP, the bottom of the page changes, allowing you to configure the parameters for static WEP.

The static WEP parameters are

- **Key Size**: Options are **not set**, **40 bits**, **104 bits**, and **128 bits**.
- **Key Index**: Options are **1** to **4**.
- **Encryption Key**: Enter the value for each key here.
- **Key Format**: Options here are **ASCII** or **HEX**.

NOTE: Each WLAN is associated with only one key index. Because only four key indexes are available, you can have only four WLANs configured for static WEP encryption.

Figure 6-13 Static WEP Configuration

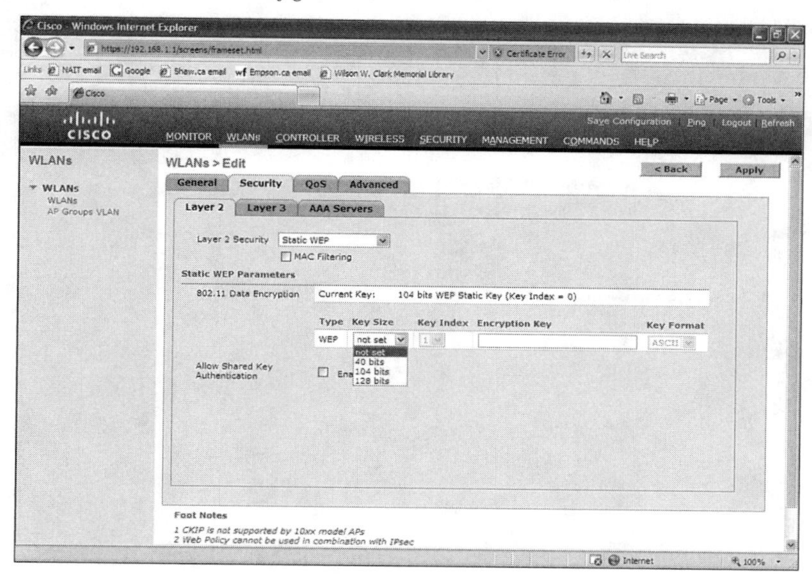

Configuring WPA with PSK

Start on the WLANs > Edit page of the WLAN you want to configure with WPA with PSK. Select the **Security** tab and on the drop-down menu for **Layer 2 Security,** choose **WPA** (or **WPA+WPA2** depending on your software) as shown in Figure 6-14. After you select **WPA** or **WPA+WPA2**, the bottom of the page changes to allow you to configure the parameters.

To set up WPA with PSK or WPA+WPA2, under the Parameters section you must select the **WPA Policy** box. For encryption, you can choose either **AES** or **TKIP**. In order to use PSK, you must select **PSK** from the drop-down menu of **Auth Key Mgmt**. The PSK Format can be either **ASCII** or **HEX**. On the last line of the Parameters section, you must enter your PSK in the long text box.

Figure 6-14 WPA with PSK Configuration

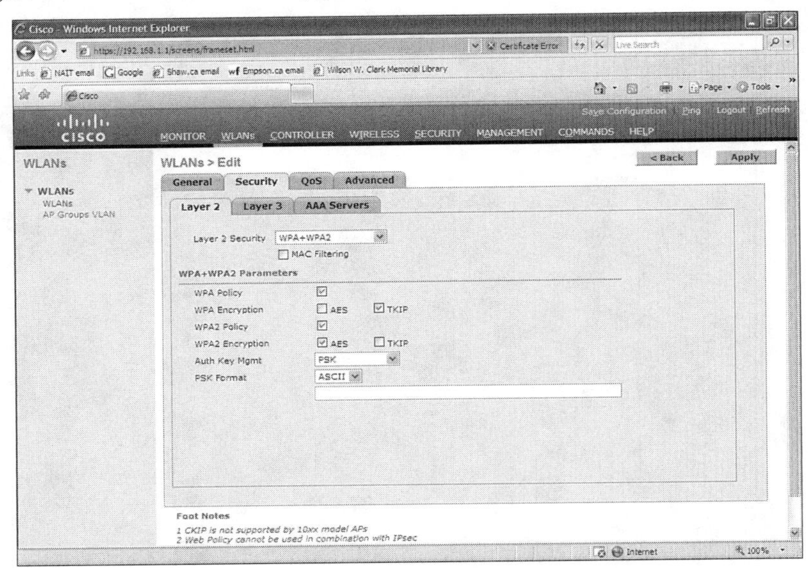

Configuring Web Authentication

Web authentication allows users to authenticate through a web browser interface. Clients who attempt to access the WLAN using HTTP are automatically redirected to a login page. The login page is customizable for both logos and text. Web authentication is usually used for guest access. The data exchanged between the client and the AP is not encrypted.

> **NOTE:** The Web Authentication feature is not available on the WLC 2000 series or the Cisco ISR WLAN Controller Modules. It is available on the WLC 4000 series and the Catalyst 6500 Series Wireless Services Module (WiSM).

> **NOTE:** The maximum simultaneous authentication requests using web authentication is 21. The maximum number of local web authentication users is 2500.

To set up web authentication, start on the WLANs > Edit page. Under the **Security** tab select the **Layer 3** tab. Check the **Web Policy** check box. When you check this box, a series of options appears, as shown in Figure 6-15. You have a choice between **Authentication** or **Passthrough**. Choosing **Authentication** prompts users for a username/password combination. Choosing **Passthrough** does not prompt the user for a username/password; you do have the choice here to select **Email Input**, which prompts the user for her email address. You can also choose an ACL to be used between the client and the controller. In Figure 6-15 no ACL has been chosen; this is shown by the word **None** in the drop-down menu for **Preauthentication ACL.**

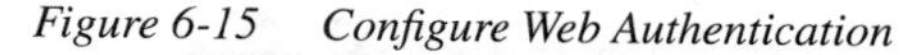

Figure 6-15 Configure Web Authentication

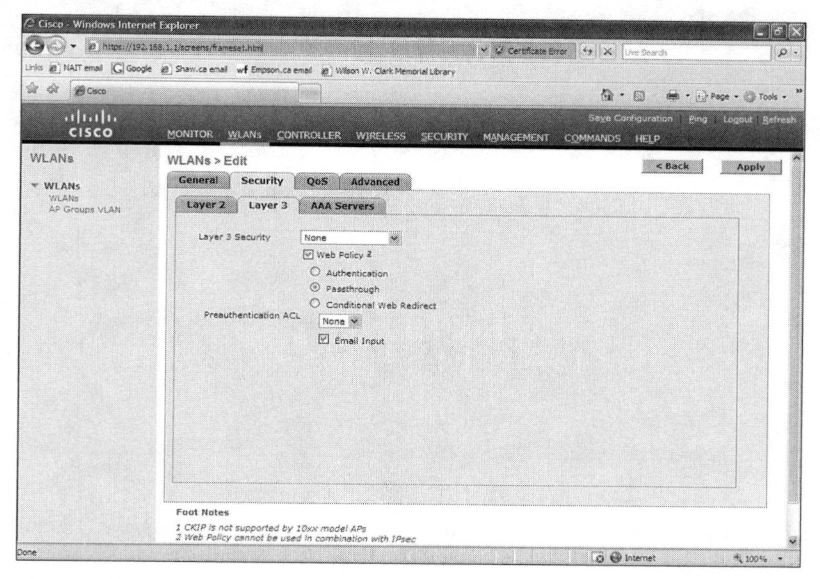

NOTE: The controller will have to reboot to load and enable the web authentication feature.

To customize the login page for web authentication, start from the main page of the WLC. Click the **Security** tab on the top of the GUI, and then click **Web Auth** on the left-side menu bar. Web Auth expands to show you the **Web Login Page** option. Click it to take you to the Web Login Page, as shown in Figure 6-16.

Figure 6-16 Web Login Page

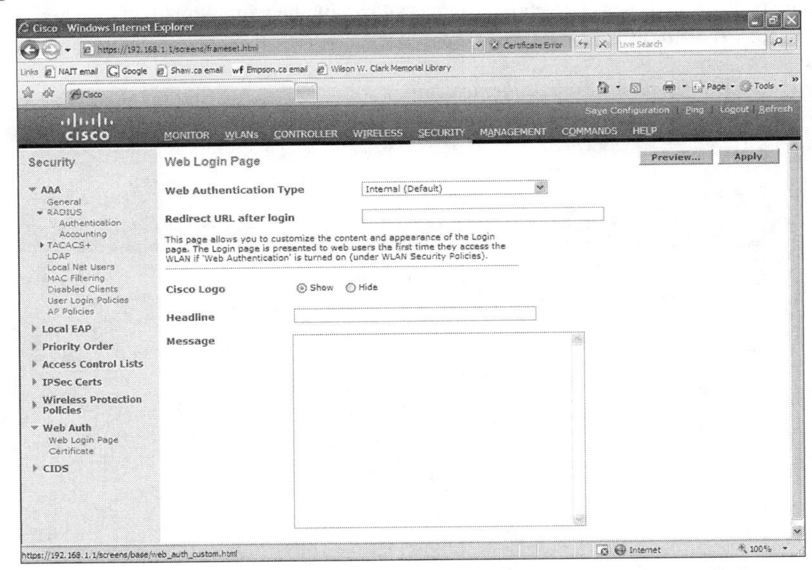

Figure 6-17 shows you the three different web authentication types: **Internal (Default)**, **Customized (Downloaded)**, and **External (Redirect to external server)**. If you choose either **External** or **Customized,** you must enter a URL in the **Redirect URL after Login** text box. In Figure 6-17 the **Redirect URL after Login** text box is hidden by the drop-down list, but it is viewable in Figure 6-16.

Configuring 802.1x Authentication

To configure 802.1x authentication, start on the WLANs > Edit page. Select **802.1x** from the **Layer 2 Security** drop-down menu in the **Layer 2** tab, as shown in Figure 6-18. After you choose 802.1x authentication, the bottom of the screen changes to show the configurable parameters for 802.1x. You can choose **MAC Filtering**, and the strength of WEP encryption as either **None**, **40 bits**, **104 bits**, or **128 bits**.

Figure 6-17 Web Authentication Types

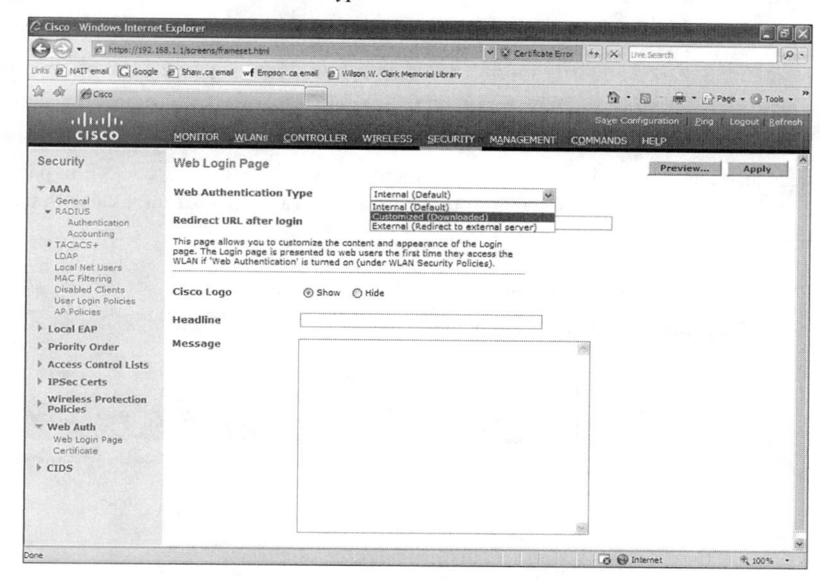

Figure 6-18 802.1x Authentication

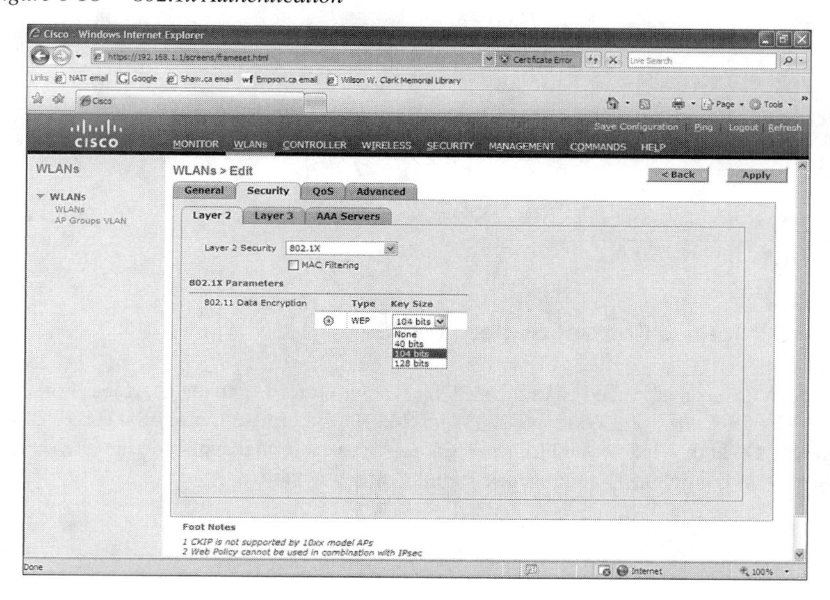

NOTE: Windows XP clients only support 40-bit or 104-bit WEP keys.

NOTE: 802.11 standards support 40/64- and 104/128-bit keys. 128/152-bit keys are supported by 802.11i, WPA, and WPA2.

You can also configure WPA with 802.1x authentication. From the WLANs > Edit page, choose the **802.1x** option from the drop-down menu for **Auth Key Mgmt**, as shown in Figure 6-19.

Figure 6-19 WPA with 802.1x Authentication

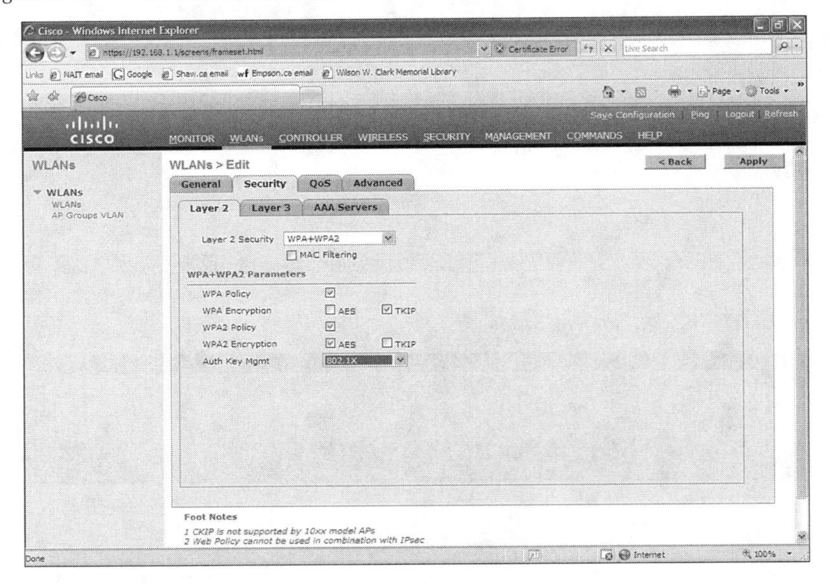

Cisco Wireless Control System (WCS)

Cisco WCS is an advanced centralized WLAN solution for Lightweight Access Points (LWAPs). WCS runs on Windows 2003 and Red Hat Enterprise Linux ES 4.0 and AS 4.0 servers. On both Windows and Linux, WCS can run as a normal application or as a service, which runs continuously and resumes running after a reboot.

The three versions of Cisco WCS are

- WCS Base
- WCS Location
- WCS Location + 2700 Series Wireless Location Appliance

NOTE: Beginning with WCS 4.1 (Windows version, or 4.0 for Linux version), both Base and Location installations are supported by the same software distribution. Which features are activated is determined by the license PAK.

WCS Login

NOTE: Cisco WCS requires Microsoft Internet Explorer 6.0 or later. Some features might not function properly if you use a web browser other than Internet Explorer 6.0 or earlier.

Using your browser software, enter the address of the WCS using the HTTPS protocol.

The login page appears, as shown in Figure 6-20. Enter your username and password, which was created during installation, and click **Login** to continue.

Figure 6-20 WCS Login Page

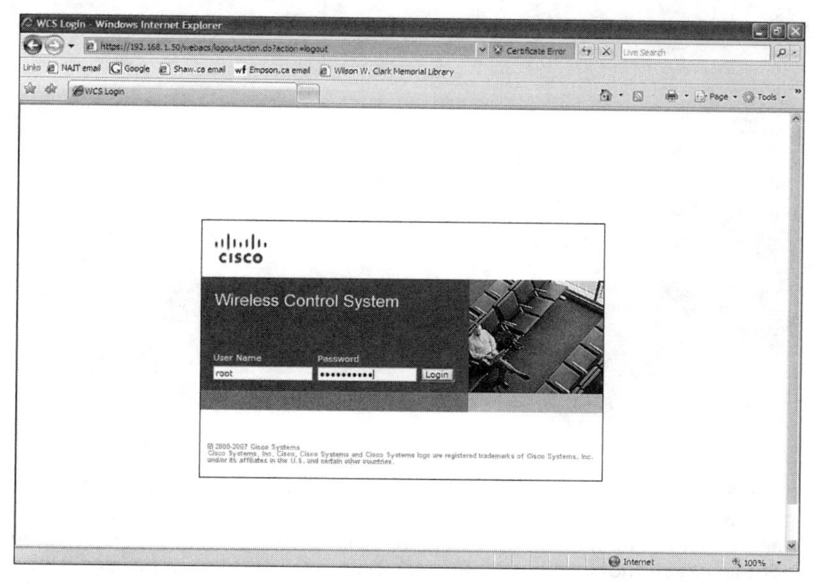

WCS Summary Pages

The GUI for WCS has different menus on each screen:

- **Monitor**: See a top-level description of all devices.
- **Reports**: View different reports on the WCS.
- **Configure**: Configure APs, controllers, and templates.

- **Location**: Configure the Cisco Wireless Location Appliances.
- **Administration**: Schedule tasks such as backups, device status, network audits, and location server synchronization.
- **Help**: Access the online help and licensing pages.

The WCS Home page is shown in Figure 6-21.

Figure 6-21 WCS Summary Pages

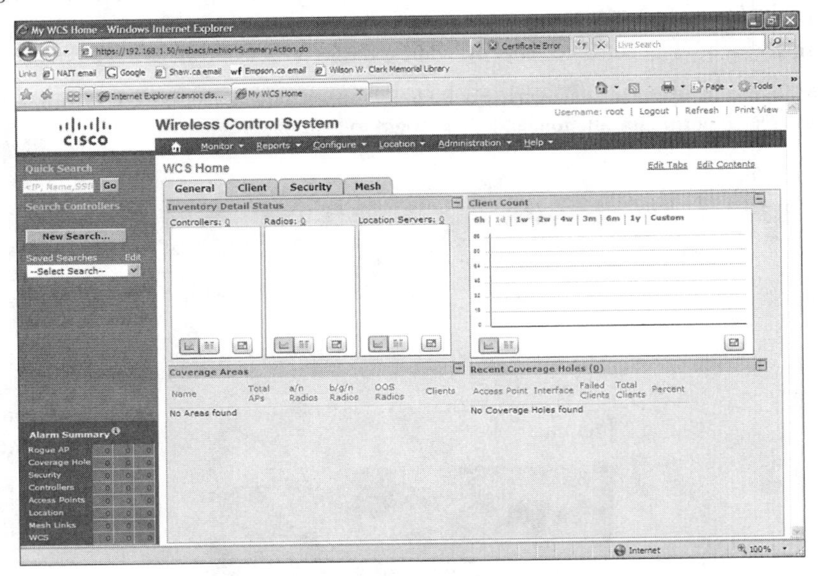

NOTE: When Cisco WCS receives an alarm from the controller, the WCS user interface displays this alarm in the lower-left corner of the screen in an area known as the Alarm Monitor. Figure 6-21 shows this as being titled Alarm Summary. These screen shots are from WCS v4.2. Older versions did not have a title for this section. Alarms can be cleared from the monitor, but the event remains. Different colors are given to help define the severity of the alarm. The alarm color codes are

Color Code	Type of Alarm
Clear	No alarm
Red	Critical alarm
Orange	Major alarm
Yellow	Minor alarm

Changing the Root Password

There are two different ways to go to the Change Password screen, where you can change the root password:

- On the top right-hand side of the screen the username of **root** is listed. Clicking that name takes you to the Change Password page.
- From the WCS Home page, click the **Administration** tab, and from the drop-down menu select **AAA**. This option takes you to the Change Password page.

The Change Password screen is shown in Figure 6-22.

Figure 6-22 Change Password for Root

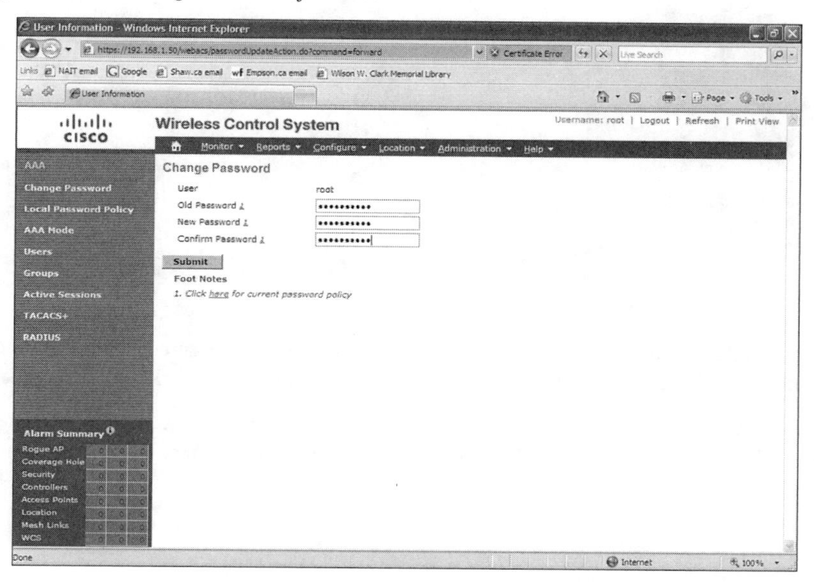

Adding a Cisco Wireless LAN Controller

To add a WLC to the WCS you must first know the IP address of the controller's service port. It is recommended that controllers be managed through the dedicated service port in order to improve security. Note that the Cisco 2000 Series WLC does not have a dedicated service port; in this case you must use the controller's management interface.

As shown in Figure 6-23, from the WCS home page, choose the **Configure** menu and then select **Controllers**.

Figure 6-23 Add a WLC

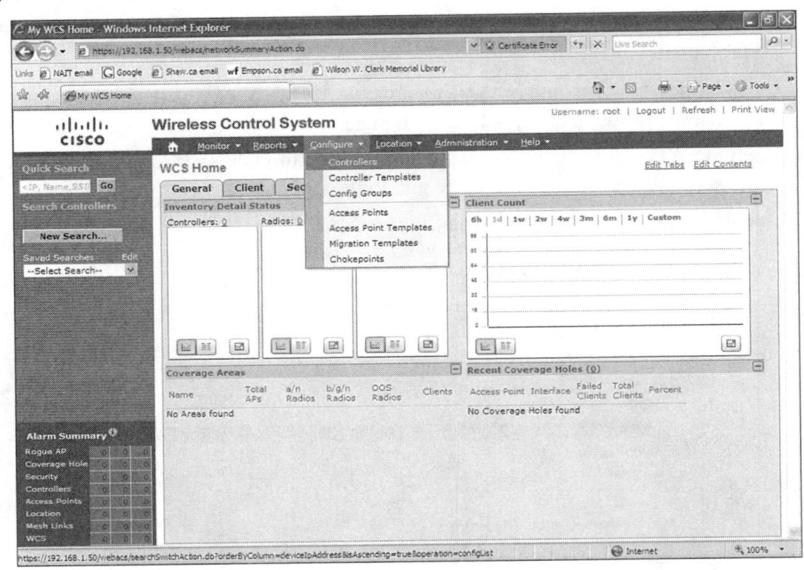

You are taken to the All Controllers Page. On the right side of the screen, choose **Add Controllers** from the drop-down menu, as shown in Figure 6-24. Click **Go** to continue.

The Add Controllers screen opens, as shown in Figure 6-25. Enter the controller IP address, network mask, and required SNMP settings. Click **OK** to continue.

Figure 6-24 Add Controllers

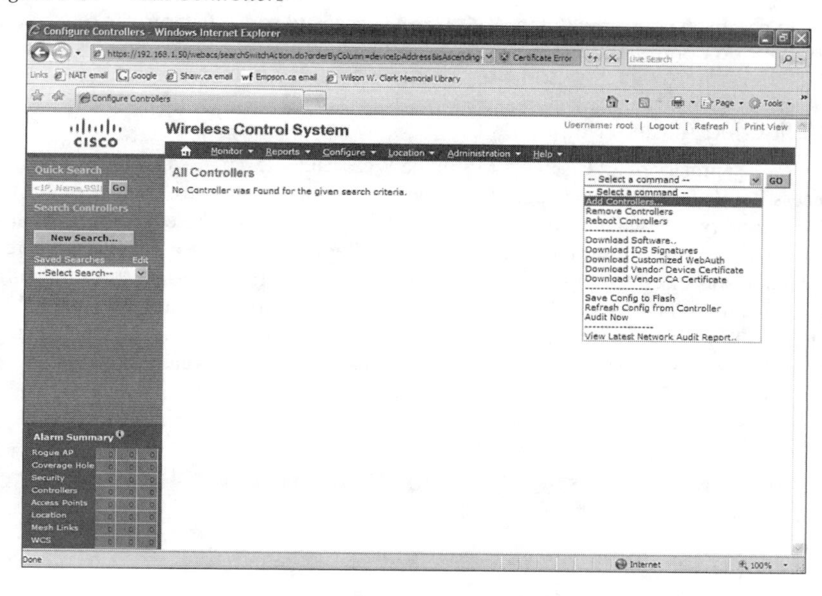

Figure 6-25 Add Controllers Page

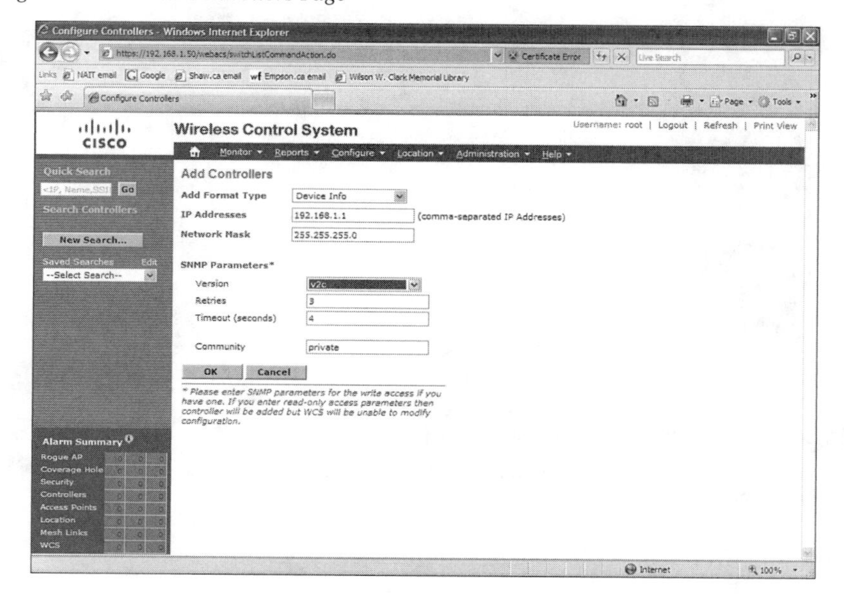

NOTE: Cisco WCS will issue a "Please Wait" dialog box while the WCS is trying to establish contact with the WLC. Upon successful contact, control is returned to the Add Controller page.

Configuring Access Points

To view a summary of all Cisco LWAPs in the WCS database, choose **Configure** and then **Access Points** from the main page. This page is shown in Figure 6-26. From here you can add third-party APs and remove Cisco LWAPs. Figure 6-26 shows these options in the drop-down menu as **Add Autonomous APs**, **Copy and Replace AP**, and **Remove APs**. There is no need to add Cisco LWAPs to the WCS database. The operating system software will automatically add Cisco LWAPs as the LWAPs associate with a WLC currently in the WCS database. The All Access Points page will display the AP name, radio type, map location, controller, port, operational status, and alarm status for all access points in the WCS database.

Figure 6-26 All Access Points Page

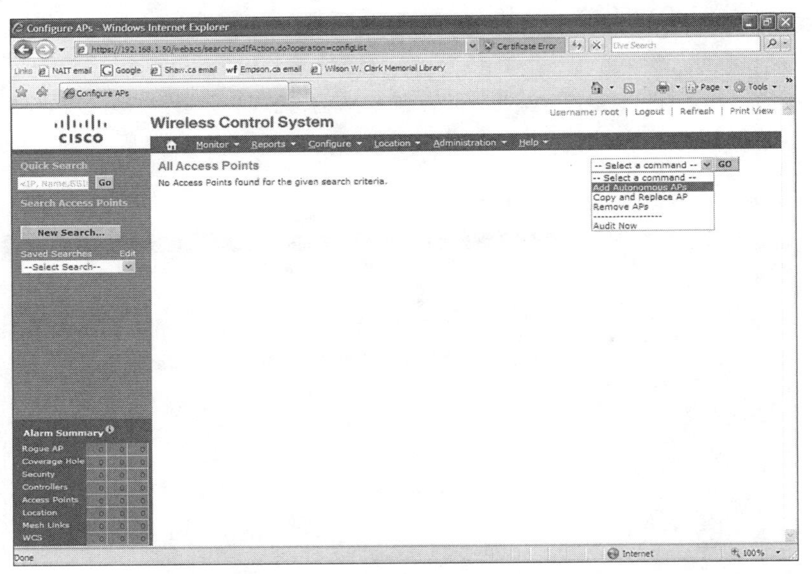

WCS Maps—Adding a Campus Map

Cisco WCS can use real floor, building, and campus plans to view the physical and RF environments together.

To add a campus map:

STEP 1. Ensure the map is in one of the following formats: .png, .jpg, .jpeg, or .gif. WCS will manage and resize the map to fit the working area.

STEP 2. Import the map from anywhere on your file system.

STEP 3. Click **Monitor** and then **Maps** to display the Maps page.

STEP 4. From the **Select a command** drop-down menu, choose **New Campus** and then click **Go**. This is shown in Figure 6-27.

Figure 6-27 Add a New Campus Map

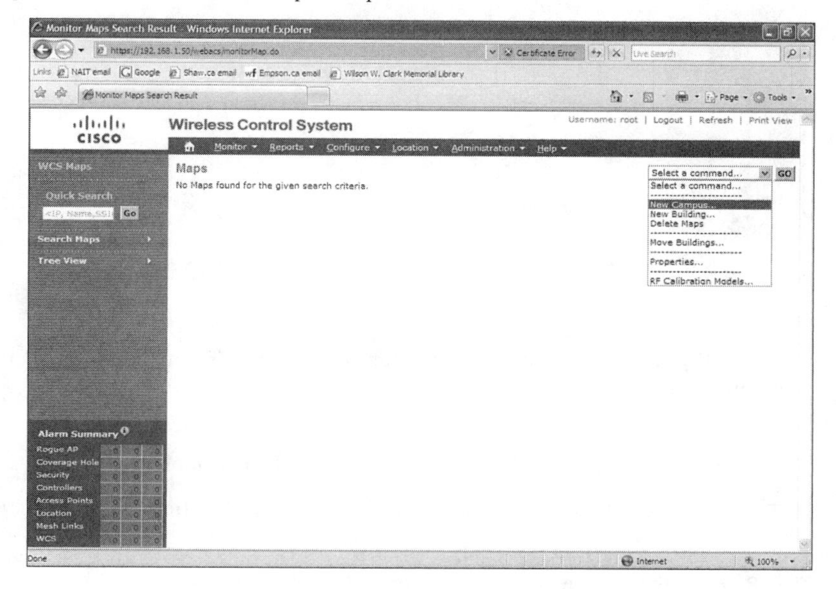

STEP 5. Enter the campus name and contact information, if wanted.

STEP 6. Browse to the campus map, as shown in Figure 6-28. Click **Next** to continue.

Figure 6-28 Browse to Campus Map

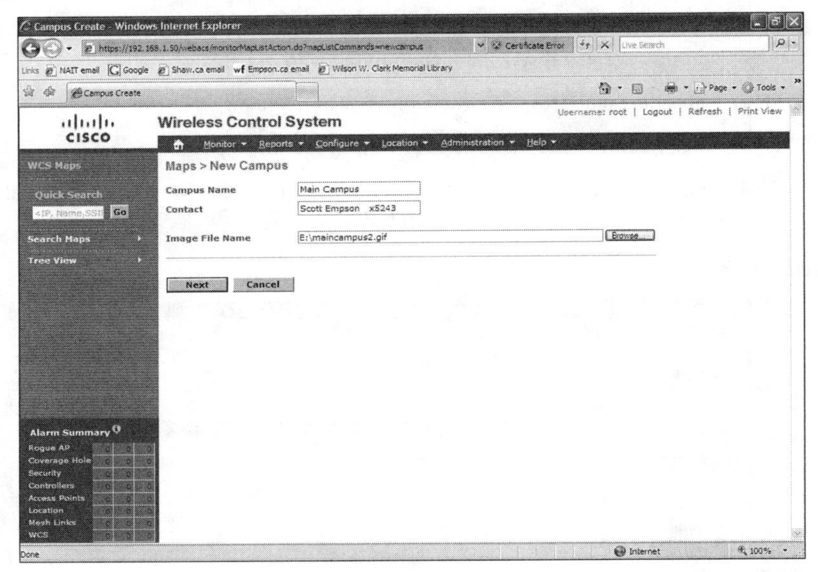

NOTE: If you are using CAD files for your maps, only DXF and DWG file images are supported.

A pop-up window will appear that will allow you to complete Steps 7 and 8.

STEP 7. Check the **Maintain Aspect Ratio** box to prevent WCS from distorting the map.

STEP 8. Enter the horizontal and vertical span of the map in feet.

Click **OK** to add this map to the WCS Database. WCS displays the Maps page, which will list maps in the database, map types, and campus status. The Maps page is shown in Figure 6-29.

Figure 6-29 Maps Page

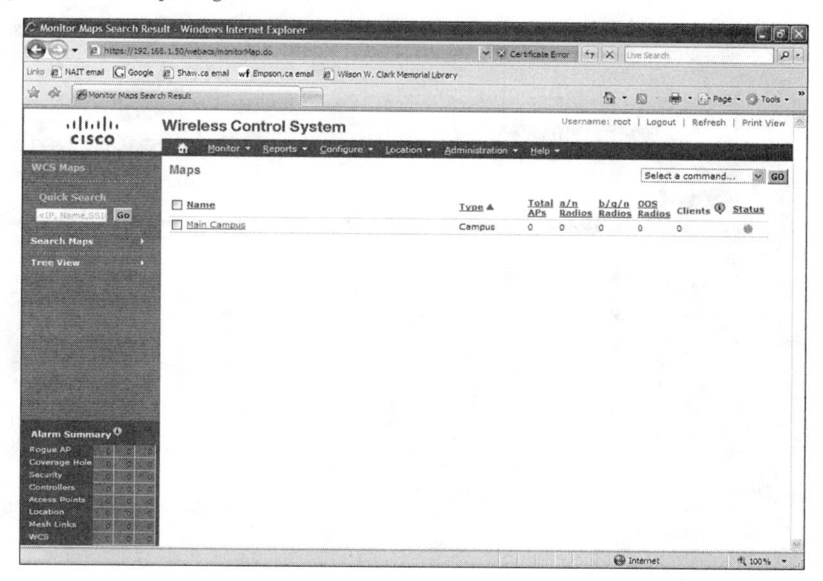

WCS Maps—Adding a New Building

You can add buildings to the WCS database, even if you have not added maps or campuses to the database.

To add a new building:

STEP 1. Click the **Monitor** tab, and then choose **Maps** to take you to the Maps page.

STEP 2. Choose the desired campus. WCS will display the Campus page, as shown in Figure 6-30.

Figure 6-30 Campus Page

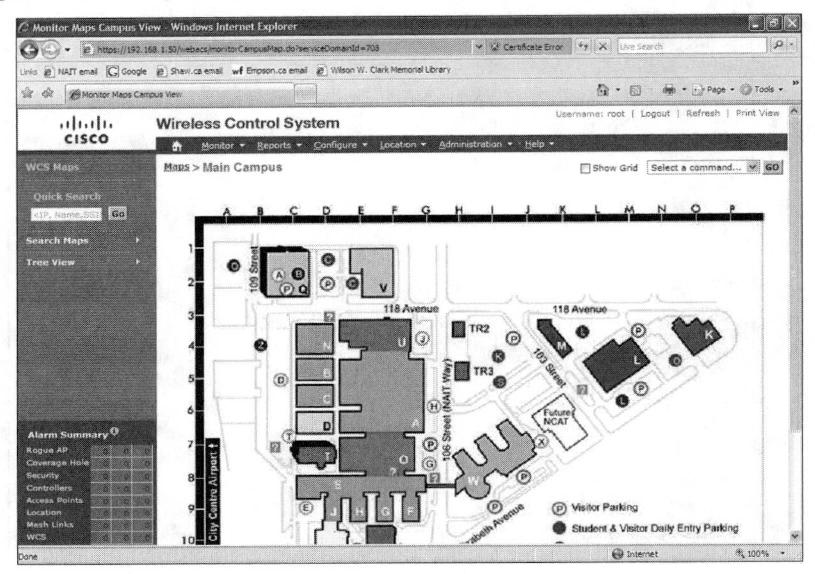

STEP 3. From the **Select a command** drop-down menu, choose **New Building** and then click **GO** to display the New Building page. You can use this option even if you do not have a map in the WCS database to start with.

STEP 4. Create a virtual building to organize related floor plan maps. You can enter the following information:

- Building name
- Contact
- Number of floors
- Number of basements
- Horizontal and vertical span size in feet

STEP 5. Click **Place** to put the building on the campus map.

STEP 6. Select the blue building rectangle and drag it to the desired location on the map. This is shown in Figure 6-31.

Figure 6-31 Create a New Building

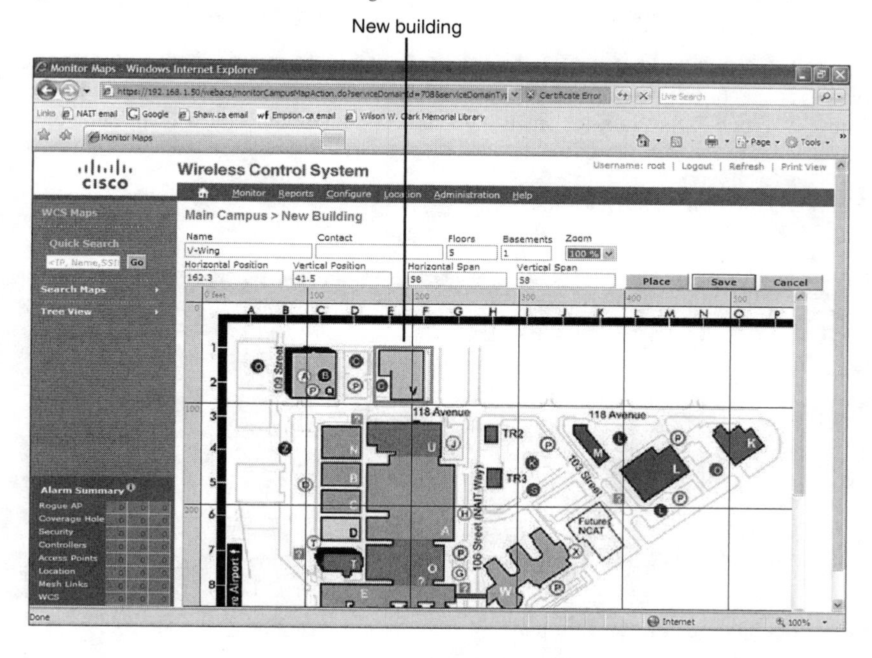

STEP 7. Click **Save**.

A hyperlink that is associated with the building will link to the corresponding Maps page.

Rogue Access Point Detection

When LWAPs are powered up and associated with controllers, Cisco WCS immediately starts listening for rogue access points. If a WLC detects a rogue access point, it notifies the WCS, which in turn creates a rogue alarm that appears in the lower-left corner of the GUI. Clicking the alarm takes you to the Rogue AP Alarms page. To browse to the Rouge AP information page, click **Monitor**, then **Alarms**, and then **Rogue AP Alarms**.

The Rogue AP Alarms page lists the following information:

- Severity
- Rogue MAC address
- Vendor
- Radio type
- Strongest AP RSSI
- Date and time

- Channel number
- SSID

To see the rogue AP calculated location on a map, choose **Map** from the Rogue AP MAC Address page, or from the menu bar choose **Monitor**, then **Maps**, followed by **Building Name**, and then **Floor Name**. A small skull and crossbones indicator will appear at the calculated location.

Figure 6-32 Rouge AP Detection

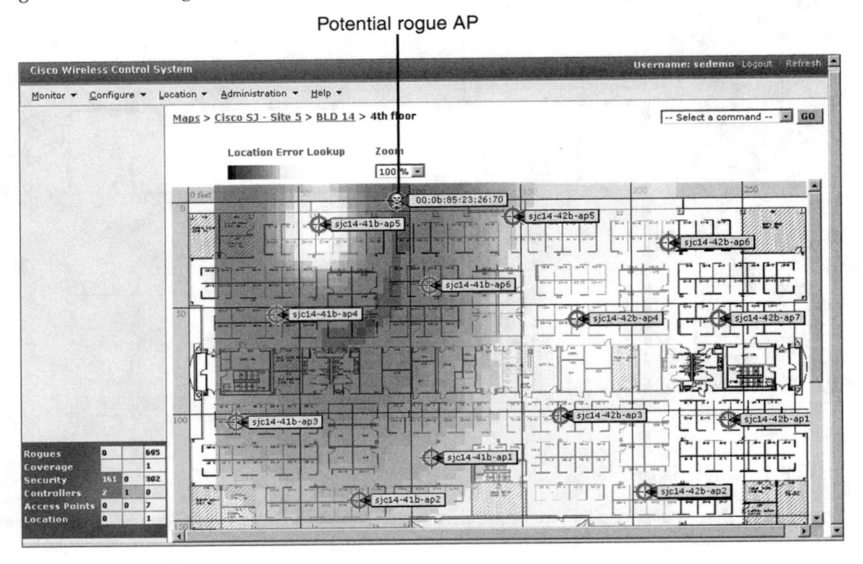

APPENDIX

Create Your Own Journal Here

Even though we have tried to be as complete as possible in this reference guide, invariably we will have left something out that you need in your specific day-to-day activities. That is why this section is here. Use these blank lines to enter in your own notes, making this reference guide your own personalized journal.